Therese Raquin

a Novel by

Emile Zola
with his Preface

with an Introduction by
Stephen R. Pastore

The Emile Zola Society
2010

The Emile Zola Society

Published by:
The Emile Zola Society
New York, NY
www.emilzolasociety.org

ISBN 13 digit: 978-0-9829579-0-5
10 digit: 0-9829579-0-4

Library of Congress Cataloging-in-Publication Data
Pastore, Stephen R.
Therese Raquin by Emile Zola/ Stephen R. Pastore, ed.
p.   cm.

First Edition

Introduction
by Stephen R. Pastore

It is one of the several failings of the American educational system that novels, poetry and plays not originally written in the English language are all but ignored by the designers of curricula. There is certainly something to be said for the failure of many translators to adequately transform a piece written in another language into English; most translators are not poets or novelists or dramatists. They tend simply to "transliterate," a term which implies the mere translation of each word as it appears in the original text without much regard for idiom, syntax or even common sense. I've seen translations of Emile Zola where the English text will read, "Stubborn, she puts on her cloak red with an abandonment of cause." This is a "literal" translation of the original French, but Zola would have been appalled as would any reader. Likely, he would have intended, "In a headstrong mood, she casually put on her red cloak." It is no wonder, then, that decision makers putting together a reading list for their students, might shun Zola (and a host of other Continental writers) despite the knowledge that he is, with little doubt, the greatest writer of the Nineteenth Century. And whether or not this is true to everyone, his significance cannot be underestimated.

There is hardly a novel written in America after Zola's work appeared that not only imitates his prose and style, but his plots as well. The term "naturalism" which came to signify an entire generation of authors from William Dean Howells through Crane and London to Dreiser, Sinclair Lewis, Faulkner and Hemingway. Even a cursory reading of biographical material on any American author writing after 1875 reveals an abiding interest in the works of Zola. Virtually everything he wrote found its way to these shores either as a pirated edition or one licensed through legal channels. Thomas Hardy, for example, easily one of the most highly admired authors, sold a few thousand copies of each of his novels on both sides of the Atlantic. His Tess of the d'Urbervilles sold about four thousand copies between its date of publication in 1886 and 1900. Zola's Nana, during that same period, sold over 200,000. Greatness, of course, is not to be measured in sales. It might even be foolish to suggest that as a criterion. But it does measure influence. Few people could seriously argue with the theory that authors tend to "run in packs." We are all familiar with the Lost Generation of writers that moved to Paris between the wars, with the Bloomsbury Group, with the Algonquin Round Table. There is a healthy symbiotic relationship that develops when creative people cavort together. They share ideas, proposals, even style. There can be no doubt whatsoever that Zola was read, re-read and discussed wherever literary minds met.

It was not just Zola's popularity that brought him to the attention of the literati. The French novel was always considered avant-garde, in the forefront of literary style and substance. While the British considered the novel as a literary form suitable only for women (men were considered the proper purveyors of "important" literature such as poetry, essays and drama), the French made no such distinction. Fanny Burney was writing her tepid novels of manners—a theme developed to its nth degree by Jane Austen—while Pierre de Laclos was penning *Les Liaisons Dangereuses* (1782) and Balzac was writing *Pere Goriot* and his *Comedie Humaine*, a monumental multi-novel series encompassing all aspects of human social behavior. Most Americans have had the good fortune to be vaguely familiar with Laclos's work through the auspices of Hollywood; the film version of the novel was a critical and popular success. Compare the novel on its most simplistic level, its plot, with Jane Austen's Pride and Prejudice written fifteen years later in 1797. When I've surveyed university students about when they thought Pride and Prejudice was written, the answers always hovered around the year 1800; the same question asked about when *Les Liaisons Dangereuses* was written, the answer was universally "sometime after 1985." It would be facile and perhaps pointless to draw conclusions from this. But the fact remains that French literature, despite its obvious influence on American literature, remains mostly un-studied and ignored. At the best, it can be blamed on faulty translations; at the worst, on a chauvinistic impulse.

Therese Raquin was published in 1867 when Zola was just 27 years old. It pre-dates his Rougon-Maquart cycle of twenty novels which was to consume most of his literary output over the next three decades of his life. It is a short novel by nineteenth century standards being only about 77,000 words, but it is truly an exercise in literary virtuosity. By anyone's standards at any time, it is a horror novel long before that term was to be used in the same sentence with greatness. The plot is simple, the number of characters quite small. A woman, Therese, is married to the son (Camille) of a headstrong woman (Madame Raquin). They re-

4

side in an apartment over a haberdashery in a dark passageway in Paris. Camille is sickly; his mother dotes over him. Therese had been a childhood friend and eventually, due to financial circumstances, finds herself marrying Camille and moving in with him and his mother; she also works at the dreary shop and her life has settled into a humdrum monotony: work, a loveless, lifeless marriage and life with a mother-in-law. The only recreation is the weekly evening visit of a group of geezers who play board games and make idle conversation. Occasionally, a young man joins the crowd, Laurent. It is inevitable that this robust, lusty man will be attracted to the submissive and wilting, yet sexually attractive, Therese.

Eventually, they have an affair, made all the more difficult by Therese's inability to get away from the shop or the watchful eye of Mama Raquin. Their sex is hurried, clandestine but animalistically passionate. Eventually, it is opined that life would be a great deal simpler if Camille were dead. In one of the great murder scenes in all literature, Camille is strangled and dumped overboard from a rowboat the three "friends" have rented for the day. (Note the similarity of this plot device to Dreiser's An American Tragedy, written in 1925.)

Eventually Laurent and Therese marry and live with Madame Raquin. The old lady has a stroke and is rendered unable to speak or move. She eventually overhears the truth about the murder of her beloved son; unable to communicate with either the murderers or the outside world she learns to watch with satisfaction the deterioration of their marriage as the "ghost" of Camille wreaks his revenge upon the doomed lovers who eventually commit a double suicide in her presence. Not content with this vision of an inner hell which is the retribution of all sinners, Zola depicts the outer hell of life in his day in Paris, a theme he continually visits in his Rougon-Macquart cycle. There is plenty of grand guignol horror as the bite which Camille inflicted on Laurent's neck in their struggle in the boat, grows, throbs and almost speaks; in the search for Camille's body in the city morgue where unclaimed bodies are put on exhibition so that loved ones may claim them, but more often, for the grisly entertainment of the public who seem to enjoy nothing better than a stroll among the gurneys where bodies in various states of undress and decay are on display.

Perhaps the greatest horror of all is reserved for Madame Raquin, who, unable to move or speak, must be nurtured and cared for by the two people who not only betrayed her trust but actively participated in her son's death. This plot line emerges in subsequent works of fiction all over the western world where people are buried alive or are physically paralyzed by drugs or restraints and made to endure atrocities (a weekly event in the television series, Dexter); in a contemporary mode, it has been recently discovered that some people under anesthesia are, in fact, wide awake to pain, but rendered inert by the drugs—a true nightmare vision which Zola has so artfully crafted in his novel. This plot device became analyzed as a mental disorder or perhaps more accurately a reaction to extreme physical disability. The term, "Locked-In Syndrome" coined by neurologist, Fred Plum in 1966:

> The first description of the locked in syndrome may not have been by a doctor but by a write—Emile Zola in Therese Raquin in 1868. Camille is murdered by Therese and her passionate, adulterous lover, Laurent. Saddened by her son's death the pitiful mother, Madame Raquin, has a stroke: "Her tongue turned to stone. Her hands and feet stiffened. She was struck dumb and motionless." After a partial respite "she had only the language of her eyes, and her niece had to guess what she wanted." Later "she could communicate quite easily with that imprisoned mind buried alive in a dead body. She had learnt to use her eyes like a hand or a mouth, to ask and give thanks, and in a strange way made up for the organs she had lost." She later discovered the lovers' treachery in murdering her son and then "made frantic efforts to . . . put all her hatred into her eyes." The wicked couple are eventually driven to take their own lives by poison. "Madame Raquin, stiff and silent, contemplated them at her feet, unable to feast her eyes enough, eyes that crushed them with brooding hate."

The triumvirate of the two doomed lovers and the hovering, wronged mother appears in Edith Wharton's *Ethan Frome* (1925). In both *Therese Raquin* and *Ethan Frome*, the true horror lies less in the acts which have led the characters to their confinement together than to the confinement itself, a sort of living hell where death seems the only escape. This is a recurrent theme in the novels of the Bronte sisters, in the novels of Somerset Maugham and later in so disparate a collection of novelists as Jerzy Kosinski, William Faulkner and Jim Crace.

Unquestionably, Zola felt attacked by most critics who savagely denounced the novel as a "mind-rotting interplay of inhuman beasts." In all likelihood, Zola would probably have agreed. But the attacks were also directed at Zola personally calling him a "pervert" and a "terrible influence on the youth of France and, indeed, all the world." The novel was a best-seller and Zola took the opportunity to defend himself in his "Preface," without in any way apologizing for the novel itself. Zola writes that he intended to "study temperaments and not characters." To his main characters, he assigns various humors according to Galen's Four Temperaments: Therese is choleric, Laurent is sanguine, and Camille is phlegmatic. For Zola, the interactions of these types of personalities could only have the result that plays out in his plot. "In a word, I wanted only one thing: given a powerful man and a dissatisfied woman, to search out the beast in them, and nothing but the beast, plunge them into a violent drama and meticulously note the feelings and actions of those two beings. I have merely performed on two living bodies the analytical work that surgeons carry out on dead ones."

Unquestionably Emile Zola created one of the most controversial novels of the Nineteenth Century when he wrote *Therese Raquin*. But this was only the beginning of a career that would extend throughout the entire century, a career that would forever alter the course of the literature of the Western world.

Therese Raquin: The Motion Picture

Zola adapted *Therese Raquin* into a play which was first staged in 1873. The play did not receive its London première until 1891, under the auspices of the Independent Theatre Society—as the Lord Chamberlain's Office refused to licence the play.

Recent stage productions include:

2006 for the Royal National Theatre, London, adaptation written by Nicholas Wright.

2007 production of the Nicholas Wright adaptation by Quantum Theatre in Pittsburgh, PA. Staged in the empty swimming pool of the Carnegie Library in Braddock, PA.

2008 production at Riverside Studios, London, adaptation by Pauline McLynn.

2009 production at Edinburgh Fringe Festival performed by pupils of The Cheltenham Ladies' College (adapted by Fiona Ross)

The novel was made into several films, including:

A 1915 silent film adaptation, which was made in Italy. It was directed by Nino Martoglio.

A 1928 German silent film

A 1953 French adaptation with Simone Signoret.

A 1956 German made-for-TV movie adaptation.

A 1965 Swedish made-for-TV movie adaptation.

A 1966 German made-for-TV movie adaptation.

A 1977 Mexican TV series adaptation.

A 1979 Belgian made-for-TV movie adaptation.

A 1980 BBC serial adaptation starring Kate Nelligan as Thérèse and Alan Rickman.

A 1985 Italian mini-series adaptation.

A 1998 BBC Radio 4 radio adaptation starring Anna Massey as Thérèse.

A 2009 BBC Radio 4 A "Classic Serial" adaptation in two parts starring Charlotte Riley as Thérèse and Andrew Buchan as Laurent.

The 2009 Korean horror film *Thirst* borrowed a number of plot elements from Thérèse Raquin.

A new film version directed by Charlie Stratton is slated for release in 2010. Actress Glenn Close is believed to also be attached to the project.

An opera based on the novel has been written by the composer Michael Finnissy. Another opera *Thérèse Raquin* by Tobias Picker opened in 2000.

The novel was also made into a Broadway musical entitled *Thou Shalt Not*, with music composition by Harry Connick, Jr.

The novel (rewritten in the style of James M. Cain) was the basis of the play "The Artificial Jungle" by Charles Ludlam.

Therese Raquin: 2010

Company Information
LumarFilm- Production Company
Liddell Entertainment - Production Company
Locations
Czech Republic
Production Credits
Director - Charlie Stratton
Screenplay - Charlie Stratton
Source Material - Emile Zola
Producer - Stefan Vorzacek
Producer - Ludvik Nemec
Producer - Mickey Liddell
Producer - Greg Berlanti
Actor - Glenn Close
Actor - Eva Green
Actor - Gerard Butler
Actor - Giovanni Ribisi
Source Material - Neal Bell
Director Of Photography - Andrew Dunn
Editor - Nigel Galt
Original Music - Michael Nyman
Casting Director - Sarah Trevis
Costume Designer - Thomas Oláh

Therese Raquin: Suggested questions for a book discussion group:

Is Therese a victim or a perpetrator?

Zola said he created temperaments not characters. Today's novels are often said to be "character driven." What is the difference between a character and a temperament?

A critic at the time the novel was written criticized Zola because he said he visited the street where the Raquin shop was located and it was sunny, bright and quite pleasant. Is this disparity relevant?

How sympathetic a character is Mrs. Raquin?

What function does the group meeting on Thursday evenings have?

Is this story realistic? Could it happen today?

There is no discussion of religion in this novel. Assuming that religion does not play a part in Zola's vision of the world, what drives Therese and Laurent to commit suicide?

For further information on *Therese Raquin* and for answers to these questions, please visit the Emile Zola Society website at www.emilezolasociety.org

ZOLA'S PREFACE TO THE
SECOND FRENCH EDITION

I had imagined in my simplicity that this novel might do without a preface. Being in the habit of saying aloud exactly what I think, of laying stress even upon the slightest details of what I write, I had hoped to have been understood and judged without any preliminary explanation. It appears that I was mistaken.

Criticism has received this book with a brutal and indignant outcry. Certain virtuous individuals, in newspapers equally virtuous, have made a grimace of disgust as they took it up with the tongs to pitch it into the fire. The little literary sheets themselves, those little sheets which chronicle every evening the news of alcoves and private supper-rooms at restaurants, have put their handkerchiefs to their noses and talked of filth and foul smells. I in nowise complain of this reception; on the contrary, I am charmed to observe that my brother journalists possess the sensitive nerves of young girls. It is quite evident that my work belongs to my judges, and that they may consider it a nauseating production without my having a right to protest. What I do complain of is that not one of the chaste journalists, who blushed on reading *Therese Raquin*, appears to me to have understood this novel. If they had understood it, perhaps they would have blushed still more, but I should at least at this moment have had the inmost satisfaction of seeing them disgusted with good cause. Nothing is more irritating than to hear worthy writers complaining of depravity, when one is intimately persuaded that they cry out without knowing their reason for doing so.

It becomes necessary, therefore, that I should myself introduce my work to my judges. I will do so in a few lines, solely with a view of avoiding all misunderstanding in the future.

In *Therese Raquin*, I have sought to study temperaments and not characters. In that lies the entire book. I have selected personages entirely dominated by their nerves and their blood, destitute of free will, led at each act of their life by the fatalities of their flesh. Therese and Laurent are human brutes, nothing more. I have sought to follow, step by step, throughout the career of these brutes, the secret working of their passions, the promptings of their instinct, the cerebral disorders following a nervous crisis. The amours of my hero and heroine are the satisfying of a necessity; the murder they commit is a consequence of their adultery, a consequence which they accept like wolves accept the slaughtering of sheep; finally, that which I have been obliged to term their remorse, consists in a simple organic disorder, in the rebellion of a nervous system strung to the point of breaking. The soul is entirely wanting; I admit this the more readily as I wished it to be so.

The reader begins, I hope, to understand that my aim has been, before all other, a scientific one. When my two personages, Therese and Laurent, were created, I took pleasure in stating certain problems to myself and in solving them; thus, I tried to explain the strange union which may be produced between two different temperaments; I showed the profound agitation of a sanguineous nature coming into contact with a nervous one. When one reads the novel carefully, one will observe that each chapter is the study of a curious case of physiology. In a word, I had but one desire: given a powerful man and an unsated woman, seek the animal within them, even see nothing but the animal, cast them into a violent drama, and scrupulously note the acts and sensations of these beings. I have simply undertaken on two living bodies the analytical work which surgeons perform on corpses.

Admit that it is hard, when one emerges from such a task, still enwrapt in the grave enjoyments of the search for truth, to hear people accuse you of having had for your sole object the painting of obscene pictures. I find myself in the same position as those painters who copy the nude, without the least desire being kindled within them, and who are profoundly surprised when a critic declares himself scandalized by the life-like flesh of their work. While engaged in writing *Therese Raquin*, I forgot the world, I became lost in the minute and exact copy of life, giving myself up entirely to the analysis of the human mechanism; and I can assure you that the cruel amours of Therese and Laurent had in them nothing immoral to my mind, nothing which could dispose one to evil passions. The humanity of the models disappeared the same as it vanishes in the eyes of the artist who has a naked woman sprawling before him, and who is solely think-ing of representing this woman on his canvas in all the truthfulness of form and color. Therefore my surprise was great when I heard my work compared to a pool of blood and mire, to a sewer, to a mass of filth, and I know not what else. I know, the pretty game of criticizing; I. have played at it myself; but I admit that the uniformity of the attack rather disconcerted me. What! There was not one of my brother writers who would explain the book, if not defend it! Among the concert of voices exclaiming, "The author of *Therese Raquin* is a wretched, hysterical being who delights in displaying obscenities," I have vainly awaited a voice that replied," Not at all! This writer is a mere analyst, who may have forgotten himself amidst human putrefaction, but who has forgotten himself there like the doctor forgets himself in the dissecting-room."

Observe that I in no way ask for the sympathy of the press for a work which, as it says, is repugnant to its delicate senses. I am not so ambitious. I am merely astonished that my brother writers should have made me out a kind of literary scavenger—they, whose experienced eyes should discover in ten pages a novelist's intentions; and I am content to humbly implore them to be good enough in future to see me as I am and to discuss me for what I am.

It was easy, though, to understand *Therese Raquin,* to place one's self on the field of observation and analysis, to show me my real faults, without going and picking up a handful of mud and throwing it in my face in the name of morality. This required only a little intelligence and a few methodical ideas in real criticism. The reproach of immoral-ity, in scientific matters, proves absolutely nothing. I do not know whether my novel is immoral; I admit that I never troubled myself to make it more or less chaste. What I do know is that I never for a moment thought of introducing into it the filth that these moral persons have discovered ; that I wrote each scene, even the most passionate, with the sole curiosity of the man of science; that I defy my judges to find in it a single page really licentious, written for the readers of those little pink books, of those indiscreet chronicles of the boudoir and the stage, which are printed ten thousand copies at a time, and warmly recommended by the very newspapers which are so disgusted by the truths in *Therese Raquin.*

A few insults, a large amount of stupidity, is therefore all I have read up to the present respecting my work. I say so here quietly, the same as I would say it to a friend who should ask me privately what I think of the attitude which criticism has taken up towards me. A writer of great talent, to whom I complained of the little sympathy I have met with, made me this profound answer: "You have an immense fault which will close all doors against you: you cannot converse for two minutes with a fool without showing him that' he is one." It must be so; I can feel the harm I do myself as regards criticism by accusing it of a want of intelligence, and yet I cannot help showing the contempt I feel for its limited horizon and the judgments it delivers with its eyes shut, without the least attempt at method. I speak, be it understood, of current criticism, of that which judges with all the literary prejudices of fools, unable to place itself on the broad, human standpoint required to understand a human work. Never before have I met with such blundering. The few blows that the minor critics have dealt me with respect to *Therese Raquin* have landed, as usual, into space. They hit, essentially, in the wrong place, applauding the capers of a powdered actress, and then complaining of immorality with reference to a physiological study, understanding nothing, unwilling to understand anything, striking always straight before them, if their panic-stricken foolishness bids them strike. It is exasperating to be beaten for a fault one has not committed. At times, I regret not having written something obscene; it seems to me that I should delight in receiving a merited castigation, in the midst of this shower of blows falling so stupidly on my head, like a cartload of bricks, without my knowing why.

In our time there are scarcely more than two or three men capable of reading, understanding, and judging a book. From these I will consent to receive lessons, persuaded as I am that they will not speak without having penetrated my intentions and appreciated the result of my efforts. They would think twice before uttering those grand empty words, morality and literary modesty; they would allow me the right, in these days of liberty in art, of choosing my subjects wherever I thought best, requiring of me no more than conscientious work, aware that folly alone is prejudicial to the dignity of letters. One thing is certain, the scientific analysis which I have attempted to perform in *Therese Raquin* would not surprise them; they would see in it the modern method, the instrument of universal inquiry of which the century makes such feverish use to penetrate the future. Whatever their conclusion might be, they would admit my point of departure, the study of temperament and of the profound modifications of organism under the pressure of circumstances and situations. I should find myself in the presence of real judges, of men honestly seeking for truth, without puerility or false shame, and not thinking it necessary to show disgust at the sight of bare and living anatomical forms. Sincere study, like fire, purifies everything.

No doubt to the tribunal I am pleased to picture at this moment my work would appear very humble; I would that it met with full severity from its critics, I would like to see it emerge black with corrections. But I should at least have the great joy of seeing myself criticized for that which I have attempted to do, and not for that which I have not done.

I can fancy I hear, even now, the sentence of high criticism, of that methodical and naturalistic criticism which has imbued science, history, and literature with new life: *Therese Raquin* is the study of too exceptional a case; the drama of modern life is more supple, less wrapped up in horror and madness. Such cases should only occupy a secondary position in a work. The desire to lose no portion of his observations has led the author to give prominence to every detail, and this has added still more tension and harshness to the whole. On the other hand, the "style does not possess the simplicity requisite in an analytical novel. It would be necessary, in short, that the writer, to enable him to construct a good novel, should see society with a wider glance, should paint it under its numerous and varied aspects, and should above all employ a plain and natural language."

I had wished to reply in twenty lines to attacks rendered irritating by their ingenuous bad faith, and I perceive that I am chatting with myself, as always happens whenever I keep a pen too long in my hand. I therefore stop, knowing that readers do not care for that kind of thing. Had I had the will and the leisure to write a manifesto, perhaps I might have attempted to defend what a journalist, speaking of *Therese Raquin*, has termed, "putrid literature." But where's the use! The group of naturalistic writers to which I have the honor to belong possesses sufficient courage and activity to produce strong works, carrying their own defense within them. It requires all the blind obstinacy of a certain class of critics to force a novelist to write a preface. As, for the sake of light, I have committed the fault of writing one, I crave the pardon of those intelligent persons who have no need to have a lamp lighted at mid-day to enable them to see clearly.

— EMILE ZOLA

CHAPTER 1

At the end of the Rue Guenegaud, coming from the quays, you find the Arcade of the Pont Neuf, a sort of narrow, dark corridor running from the Rue Mazarine to the Rue de Seine. This arcade, at the most, is thirty paces long by two in breadth. It is paved with worn, loose, yellowish tiles which are never free from acrid damp. The square panes of glass forming the roof, are black with filth.

On fine days in the summer, when the streets are burning with heavy sun, whitish light falls from the dirty glazing overhead to drag miserably through the arcade. On nasty days in winter, on foggy mornings, the glass throws nothing but darkness on the sticky tiles—unclean and abominable gloom.

To the left are obscure, low, dumpy shops whence issue puffs of air as cold as if coming from a cellar. Here are dealers in toys, cardboard boxes, second-hand books. The articles displayed in their windows are covered with dust, and owing to the prevailing darkness, can only be perceived indistinctly. The shop fronts, formed of small panes of glass, streak the goods with a peculiar greenish reflex. Beyond, behind the display in the windows, the dim interiors resemble a number of lugubrious cavities animated by fantastic forms.

To the right, along the whole length of the arcade, extends a wall against which the shopkeepers opposite have stuck some small cupboards. Objects without a name, goods forgotten for twenty years, are spread out there on thin shelves painted a horrible brown colour. A dealer in imitation jewelry, has set up shop in one of these cupboards, and there sells fifteen sous rings, delicately set out on a cushion of blue velvet at the bottom of a mahogany box.

Above the glazed cupboards, ascends the roughly plastered black wall, looking as if covered with leprosy, and all seamed with defacements.

The Arcade of the Pont Neuf is not a place for a stroll. You take it to make a short cut, to gain a few minutes. It is traversed by busy people whose sole aim is to go quick and straight before them. You see apprentices there in their working-aprons, work-girls taking home their work, persons of both sexes with parcels under their arms. There are also old men who drag themselves forward in the sad gloaming that falls from the glazed roof, and bands of small children who come to the arcade on leaving school, to make a noise by stamping their feet on the tiles as they run along. Throughout the day a sharp hurried ring of footsteps, resounds on the stone with irritating irregularity. Nobody speaks, nobody stays there, all hurry about their business with bent heads, stepping out rapidly, without taking a single glance at the shops. The tradesmen observe with an air of alarm, the passers-by who by a miracle stop before their windows.

The arcade is lit at night by three gas burners, enclosed in heavy square lanterns. These jets of gas, hanging from the glazed roof whereon they cast spots of fawn-coloured light, shed around them circles of pale glimmer that seem at moments to disappear. The arcade now assumes the aspect of a regular cut-throat alley. Great shadows stretch along the tiles, damp puffs of air enter from the street. Anyone might take the place for a subterranean gallery indistinctly lit-up by three funeral lamps. The tradespeople for all light are contented with the faint rays which the gas burners throw upon their windows. Inside their shops, they merely have a lamp with a shade, which they place at the corner of their counter, and the passer-by can then distinguish what the depths of these holes sheltering night in the daytime, contain. On this blackish line of shop fronts, the windows of a cardboard-box maker are flaming: two schist-lamps pierce the shadow with a couple of yellow flames. And, on the other side of the arcade a candle, stuck in the middle of an argand lamp glass, casts glistening stars into the box of imitation jewelry. The dealer is dozing in her cupboard, with her hands hidden under her shawl.

A few years back, opposite this dealer, stood a shop whose bottle-green woodwork excreted damp by all its cracks. On the signboard, made of a long narrow plank, figured, in black letters the word: HABERDASHER. And on one of the panes of glass in the door was written, in red, the name of a woman: *Therese Raquin*. To right and left were deep show cases, lined with blue paper.

During the daytime the eye could only distinguish the display of goods, in a soft, obscured light.

On one side were a few linen articles: crimped tulle caps at two and three francs apiece, muslin sleeves and collars: then undervests, stockings, socks, braces. Each article had grown yellow and crumpled, and hung lamentably suspended from a wire hook. The window, from top to bottom, was filled in this manner with whitish bits of clothing, which took a lugubrious aspect in the transparent obscurity. The new caps, of brighter whiteness, formed hollow spots on the blue paper covering the shelves. And the coloured socks hanging on an iron rod, contributed sombre notes to the livid and vague effacement of the muslin.

On the other side, in a narrower show case, were piled up large balls of green wool, white cards of black buttons, boxes of all colours and sizes, hair nets ornamented with steel beads, spread over rounds of bluish paper, fasces of knitting needles, tapestry patterns, bobbins of ribbon, along with a heap of soiled and faded articles, which doubtless had been lying in the same place for five or six years. All the tints had turned dirty grey in this cupboard, rotting with dust and damp.

In summer, towards noon, when the sun scorched the squares and streets with its tawny rays, you could distinguish, behind the caps in the other window, the pale, grave profile of a young woman. This profile issued vaguely from the darkness reigning in the shop. To a low parched forehead was attached a long, narrow, pointed nose; the pale pink lips resembled two thin threads, and the short, nervy chin was attached to the neck by a line that was supple and fat. The body, lost in the shadow, could not be seen. The profile alone appeared in its olive whiteness, perforated by a large, wide-open, black eye, and as though crushed beneath thick dark hair. This profile remained there for hours, motionless and peaceful, between a couple of caps for women, whereon the damp iron rods had imprinted bands of rust.

At night, when the lamp had been lit, you could see inside the shop which was greater in length than depth. At one end stood a small counter; at the other, a corkscrew staircase afforded communication with the rooms on the first floor. Against the walls were show cases, cupboards, rows of green cardboard boxes. Four chairs and a table completed the furniture. The shop looked bare and frigid; the goods were done up in parcels and put away in corners instead of lying hither and thither in a joyous display of colour.

As a rule two women were seated behind the counter: the young woman with the grave profile, and an old lady who sat dozing with a smile on her countenance. The latter was about sixty; and her fat, placid face looked white in the brightness of the lamp. A great tabby cat, crouching at a corner of the counter, watched her as she slept.

Lower down, on a chair, a man of thirty sat reading or chatting in a subdued voice with the young woman. He was short, delicate, and in manner languid. With his fair hair devoid of lustre, his sparse beard, his face covered with red blotches, he resembled a sickly, spoilt child arrived at manhood.

Shortly before ten o'clock, the old lady awoke. The shop was then closed, and all the family went upstairs to bed. The tabby cat followed the party purring, and rubbing its head against each bar of the banisters.

The lodging above comprised three apartments. The staircase led to a dining-room which also did duty as drawing-room. In a niche on the left stood a porcelain stove; opposite, a sideboard; then chairs were arranged along the walls, and a round table occupied the centre. At the further end a glazed partition concealed a dark kitchen. On each side of the dining-room was a sleeping apartment.

The old lady after kissing her son and daughter-in-law withdrew. The cat went to sleep on a chair in the kitchen. The married couple entered their room, which had a second door opening on a staircase that communicated with the arcade by an obscure narrow passage.

The husband who was always trembling with fever went to bed, while the young woman opened the window to close the shutter blinds. She remained there a few minutes facing the great black wall, which ascends and stretches above the arcade. She cast a vague wandering look upon this wall, and, without a word she, in her turn, went to bed in disdainful indifference.

CHAPTER II

Madame Raquin had formerly been a mercer at Vernon. For close upon five-and-twenty years, she had kept a small shop in that town. A few years after the death of her husband, becoming subject to fits of faintness, she sold her business. Her savings added to the price of this sale placed a capital of 40,000 francs in her hand which she invested so that it brought her in an income of 2,000 francs a year. This sum amply sufficed for her requirements. She led the life of a recluse. Ignoring the poignant joys and cares of this world, she arranged for herself a tranquil existence of peace and happiness.

At an annual rental of 400 francs she took a small house with a garden descending to the edge of the Seine. This enclosed, quiet residence vaguely recalled the cloister. It stood in the centre of large fields, and was approached by a narrow path. The windows of the dwelling opened to the river and to the solitary hillocks on the opposite bank. The good lady, who had passed the half century, shut herself up in this solitary retreat, where along with her son Camille and her niece Therese, she partook of serene joy.

Although Camille was then twenty, his mother continued to spoil him like a little child. She adored him because she had shielded him from death, throughout a tedious childhood of constant suffering. The boy contracted every fever, every imaginable malady, one after the other. Madame Raquin struggled for fifteen years against these terrible evils, which arrived in rapid succession to tear her son away from her. She vanquished them all by patience, care, and adoration. Camille having grown up, rescued from death, had contracted a shiver from the torture of the repeated shocks he had undergone. Arrested in his growth, he remained short and delicate. His long, thin limbs moved slowly and wearily. But his mother loved him all the more on account of this weakness that arched his back. She observed his thin, pale face with triumphant tenderness when she thought of how she had brought him back to life more than ten times over.

During the brief spaces of repose that his sufferings allowed him, the child attended a commercial school at Vernon. There he learned orthography and arithmetic. His science was limited to the four rules, and a very superficial knowledge of grammar. Later on, he took lessons in writing and bookkeeping. Madame Raquin began to tremble when advised to send her son to college. She knew he would die if separated from her, and she said the books would kill him. So Camille remained ignorant, and this ignorance seemed to increase his weakness.

At eighteen, having nothing to do, bored to death at the delicate attention of his mother, he took a situation as clerk with a linen merchant, where he earned 60 francs a month. Being of a restless nature idleness proved unbearable. He found greater calm and better health in this labour of a brute which kept him bent all day long over invoices, over enormous additions, each figure of which he patiently added up. At night, broken down with fatigue, without an idea in his head, he enjoyed infinite delight in the doltishness that settled on him. He had to quarrel with his mother to go with the dealer in linen. She wanted to keep him always with her, between a couple of blankets, far from the accidents of life.

But the young man spoke as master. He claimed work as children claim toys, not from a feeling of duty, but by instinct, by a necessity of nature. The tenderness, the devotedness of his mother had instilled into him an egotism that was ferocious. He fancied he loved those who pitied and caressed him; but, in reality, he lived apart, within himself, loving naught but his comfort, seeking by all possible means to increase his enjoyment. When the tender affection of Madame Raquin disgusted him, he plunged with delight into a stupid occupation that saved him from infusions and potions.

In the evening, on his return from the office, he ran to the bank of the Seine with his cousin Therese who was then close upon eighteen. One day, sixteen years previously, while Madame Raquin was still a mercer, her brother Captain Degans brought her a little girl in his arms. He had just arrived from Algeria.

"Here is a child," said he with a smile, "and you are her aunt. The mother is dead and I don't know what to do with her. I'll give her to you."

The mercer took the child, smiled at her and kissed her rosy cheeks. Although Degans remained a week at Vernon, his sister barely put a question to him concerning the little girl he had brought her. She understood vaguely that the dear little creature was born at Oran, and that her mother was a woman of the country of great beauty. The Captain, an hour before his departure, handed his sister a certificate of birth in which Therese, acknowledged by him to be his child, bore his name. He rejoined his regiment, and was never seen again at Vernon, being killed a few years later in Africa.

Therese grew up under the fostering care of her aunt, sleeping in the same bed as Camille. She who had an iron constitution, received the treatment of a delicate child, partaking of the same medicine as her cousin, and kept in the warm air of the room occupied by the invalid. For hours she remained crouching over the fire, in thought, watching the flames before her, without lowering her eyelids.

This obligatory life of a convalescent caused her to retire within herself. She got into the habit of talking in a low voice, of moving about noiselessly, of remaining mute and motionless on a chair with expressionless, open eyes. But, when she raised an arm, when she advanced a foot, it was easy to perceive that she possessed feline suppleness, short, potent muscles, and that unmistakable energy and passion slumbered in her soporous frame. Her cousin having fallen down one day in a fainting fit, she abruptly picked him up and carried him—an effort of strength that turned her cheeks scarlet. The cloistered life she led, the debilitating regimen to which she found herself subjected, failed to weaken her thin, robust form. Only her face took a pale, and even a slightly yellowish tint, making her look almost ugly in the shade. Ever and anon she went to the window, and contemplated the opposite houses on which the sun threw sheets of gold.

When Madame Raquin sold her business, and withdrew to the little place beside the river, Therese experienced secret thrills of joy. Her aunt had so frequently repeated to her: "Don't make a noise; be quiet," that she kept all the impetuosity of her nature carefully concealed within her. She possessed supreme composure, and an apparent tranquillity that masked terrible transports. She still fancied herself in the room of her cousin, beside a dying child, and had the softened movements, the periods of silence, the placidity, the faltering speech of an old woman.

When she saw the garden, the clear river, the vast green hillocks ascending on the horizon, she felt a savage desire to run and shout. She felt her heart thumping fit to burst in her bosom; but not a muscle of her face moved, and she merely smiled when her aunt inquired whether she was pleased with her new home.

Life now became more pleasant for her. She maintained her supple gait, her calm, indifferent countenance, she remained the child brought up in the bed of an invalid; but inwardly she lived a burning, passionate existence. When alone on the grass beside the water, she would lie down flat on her stomach like an animal, her black eyes wide open, her body writhing, ready to spring. And she stayed there for hours, without a thought, scorched by the sun, delighted at being able to thrust her fingers in the earth. She had the most ridiculous dreams; she looked at the roaring river in defiance, imagining that the water was about to leap on her and attack her. Then she became rigid, preparing for the defence, and angrily inquiring of herself how she could vanquish the torrent.

At night, Therese, appeased and silent, stitched beside her aunt, with a countenance that seemed to be dozing in the gleam that softly glided from beneath the lamp shade. Camille buried in an armchair thought of his additions. A word uttered in a low voice, alone disturbed, at moments, the peacefulness of this drowsy home.

Madame Raquin observed her children with serene benevolence. She had resolved to make them husband and wife. She continued to treat her son as if he were at death's door; and she trembled when she happened to reflect that she would one day die herself, and would leave him alone and suffering. In that contingency, she relied on Therese, saying to herself that the young girl would be a vigilant guardian beside Camille. Her niece with her tranquil manner, and mute devotedness, inspired her with unlimited confidence. She had seen Therese at work, and wished to give her to her son as a guardian angel. This marriage was a solution to the matter, foreseen and settled in her mind.

The children knew for a long time that they were one day to marry. They had grown up with this idea, which had thus become familiar and natural to them. The union was spoken of in the family as a necessary and positive thing. Madame Raquin had said:

"We will wait until Therese is one-and-twenty."

And they waited patiently, without excitement, and without a blush.

Camille, whose blood had become impoverished by illness, had remained a little boy in the eyes of his cousin. He kissed her as he kissed his mother, by habit, without losing any of his egotistic tranquillity. He looked upon her as an obliging comrade who helped him to amuse himself, and who, if occasion offered, prepared him an infusion. When playing with her, when he held her in his arms, it was as if he had a boy to deal with. He experienced no thrill, and at these moments the idea had never occurred to him of planting a warm kiss on her lips as she struggled with a nervous laugh to free herself.

The girl also seemed to have remained cold and indifferent. At times her great eyes rested on Camille and fixedly gazed at him with sovereign calm. On such occasions her lips alone made almost imperceptible little motions. Nothing could be read on her expressionless countenance, which an inexorable will always maintained gentle and attentive. Therese became grave when the conversation turned to her marriage, contenting herself with approving all that Madame Raquin said by a sign of the head. Camille went to sleep.

On summer evenings, the two young people ran to the edge of the water. Camille, irritated at the incessant attentions of his mother, at times broke out in open revolt. He wished to run about and make himself ill, to escape the fondling that disgusted him. He would then drag Therese along with him, provoking her to wrestle, to roll in the grass. One day, having pushed his cousin down, the young girl bounded to her feet with all the savageness of a wild beast, and, with flaming face and bloodshot eyes, fell upon him with clenched fists. Camille in fear sank to the ground.

Months and years passed by, and at length the day fixed for the marriage arrived. Madame Raquin took Therese apart, spoke to her of her father and mother, and related to her the story of her birth. The young girl listened to her aunt, and when she had finished speaking, kissed her, without answering a word.

At night, Therese, instead of going into her own room, which was on the left of the staircase, entered that of her cousin which was on the right. This was all the change that occurred in her mode of life. The following day, when the young couple came downstairs, Camille had still his sickly languidness, his righteous tranquillity of an egotist. Therese still maintained her gentle indifference, and her restrained expression of frightful calmness.

CHAPTER III

A week after the marriage, Camille distinctly told his mother that he intended quitting Vernon to reside in Paris. Madame Raquin protested: she had arranged her mode of life, and would not modify it in any way. Thereupon her son had a nervous attack, and threatened to fall ill, if she did not give way to his whim.

"Never have I opposed you in your plans," said he; "I married my cousin, I took all the drugs you gave me. It is only natural, now, when I have a desire of my own, that you should be of the same mind. We will move at the end of the month."

Madame Raquin was unable to sleep all night. The decision Camille had come to, upset her way of living, and, in despair, she sought to arrange another existence for herself and the married couple. Little by little, she recovered calm. She reflected that the young people might have children, and that her small fortune would not then suffice. It was necessary to earn money, to go into business again, to find lucrative occupation for Therese. The next day she had become accustomed to the idea of moving, and had arranged a plan for a new life.

At luncheon she was quite gay.

"This is what we will do," said she to her children. "I will go to Paris to-morrow. There I will look out for a small mercery business for sale, and Therese and myself will resume selling needles and cotton, which will give us something to do. You, Camille, will act as you like. You can either stroll about in the sun, or you can find some employment."

"I shall find employment," answered the young man.

The truth was that an idiotic ambition had alone impelled Camille to leave Vernon. He wished to find a post in some important administration. He blushed with delight when he fancied he saw himself in the middle of a large office, with lustring elbow sleeves, and a pen behind his ear.

Therese was not consulted: she had always displayed such passive obedience that her aunt and husband no longer took the trouble to ask her opinion. She went where they went, she did what they did, without a complaint, without a reproach, without appearing even to be aware that she changed her place of residence.

Madame Raquin came to Paris, and went straight to the Arcade of the Pont Neuf. An old maid at Vernon had sent her to one of her relatives who in this arcade kept a mercery shop which she desired to get rid of. The former mercer found the shop rather small, and rather dark; but, in passing through Paris, she had been taken aback by the noise in the streets, by the luxuriously dressed windows, and this narrow gallery, this modest shop front, recalled her former place of business which was so peaceful. She could fancy herself again in the provinces, and she drew a long breath thinking that her dear children would be happy in this out-of-the-way corner. The low price asked for the business, caused her to make up her mind. The owner sold it her for 2,000 francs, and the rent of the shop and first floor was only 1,200 francs a year. Madame Raquin, who had close upon 4,000 francs saved up, calculated that she could pay for the business and settle the rent for the first year, without encroaching on her fortune. The salary Camille would be receiving, and the profit on the mercery business would suffice, she thought, to meet the daily expenses; so that she need not touch the income of her funded money, which would capitalise, and go towards providing marriage portions for her grandchildren.

She returned to Vernon beaming with pleasure, relating that she had found a gem, a delightful little place right in the centre of Paris. Little by little, at the end of a few days, in her conversations of an evening, the damp, obscure shop in the arcade became a palace; she pictured it to herself, so far as her memory served her, as convenient, spacious, tranquil, and replete with a thousand inestimable advantages.

"Ah! my dear Therese," said she, "you will see how happy we shall be in that nook! There are three beautiful rooms upstairs. The arcade is full of people. We will make charming displays. There is no fear of our feeling dull."

But she did not stop there. All her instinct of a former shopkeeper was awakened. She gave advice to Therese, beforehand, as to buying and selling, and posted her up in all the tricks of small tradespeople. At length, the family quitted the house beside the Seine, and on the evening of the same day, were installed in the Arcade of the Pont Neuf.

When Therese entered the shop, where in future she was to live, it seemed to her that she was descending into the clammy soil of a grave. She felt quite disheartened, and shivered with fear. She looked at the dirty, damp gallery, visited the shop, and ascending to the first floor, walked round each room. These bare apartments, without furniture, looked frightful in their solitude and dilapidation. The young woman could not make a gesture, or utter a word. She was as if frozen. Her aunt and husband having come downstairs, she seated herself on a trunk, her hands rigid, her throat full of sobs, and yet she could not cry.

Madame Raquin, face to face with reality, felt embarrassed, and ashamed of her dreams. She sought to defend her acquisition. She found a remedy for every fresh inconvenience that was discovered, explaining the obscurity by saying the weather was overcast, and concluded by affirming that a sweep-up would suffice to set everything right.

"Bah!" answered Camille, "all this is quite suitable. Besides, we shall only come up here at night. I shall not be home before five or six o'clock. As to you two, you will be together, so you will not be dull."

The young man would never have consented to inhabit such a den, had he not relied on the comfort of his office. He said to himself that he would be warm all day at his administration, and that, at night, he would go to bed early.

For a whole week, the shop and lodging remained in disorder. Therese had seated herself behind the counter from the first day, and she did not move from that place. Madame Raquin was astonished at this depressed attitude. She had thought that the young woman would try to adorn her habitation. That she would place flowers at the windows, and ask for new papers, curtains and carpets. When she suggested some repairs, some kind of embellishment, her niece quietly replied:

"What need is there for it? We are very well as we are. There is no necessity for luxury."

It was Madame Raquin who had to arrange the rooms and tidy up the shop. Therese at last lost patience at seeing the good old lady incessantly turning round and round before her eyes; she engaged a charwoman, and forced her aunt to be seated beside her.

Camille remained a month without finding employment. He lived as little as possible in the shop, preferring to stroll about all day; and he found life so dreadfully dull with nothing to do, that he spoke of returning to Vernon. But he at length obtained a post in the administration of the Orleans Railway, where he earned 100 francs a month. His dream had become realised.

He set out in the morning at eight o'clock. Walking down the Rue Guenegaud, he found himself on the quays. Then, taking short steps with his hands in his pockets, he followed the Seine from the Institut to the Jardin des Plantes. This long journey which he performed twice daily, never wearied him. He watched the water running along, and he stopped to see the rafts of wood descending the river, pass by. He thought of nothing. Frequently he planted himself before Notre Dame, to contemplate the scaffolding surrounding the cathedral which was then undergoing repair. These huge pieces of timber amused him although he failed to understand why. Then he cast a glance into the Port aux Vins as he went past, and after that counted the cabs coming from the station.

In the evening, quite stupefied, with his head full of some silly story related to his office, he crossed the Jardin des Plantes, and went to have a look at the bears, if he was not in too great a hurry. There he remained half an hour, leaning over the rails at the top of the pit, observing the animals clumsily swaying to and fro. The behaviour of these huge beasts pleased him. He examined them with gaping mouth and rounded eyes, partaking of the joy of an idiot when he perceived them bestir themselves. At last he turned homewards, dragging his feet along, busying himself with the passers-by, with the vehicles, and the shops.

As soon as he arrived he dined, and then began reading. He had purchased the works of Buffon, and, every evening, he set himself to peruse twenty to thirty pages, notwithstanding the wearisome nature of the task. He also read in serial, at 10 centimes the number, "The History of the Consulate and Empire" by Thiers, and "The History of the Girondins" by Lamartine, as well as some popular scientific works. He fancied he was labouring at his education. At times, he forced his wife to listen to certain pages, to particular anecdotes, and felt very much astonished that Therese could remain pensive and silent the whole evening, without being tempted to take up a book. And he thought to himself that his wife must be a woman of very poor intelligence.

Therese thrust books away from her with impatience. She preferred to remain idle, with her eyes fixed, and her thoughts wandering and lost. But she maintained an even, easy temper, exercising all her will to render herself a passive instrument, replete with supreme complaisance and abnegation.

The shop did not do much business. The profit was the same regularly each month. The customers consisted of female workpeople living in the neighbourhood. Every five minutes a young girl came in to purchase a few sous worth of goods. Therese served the people with words that were ever the same, with a smile that appeared mechanically on her lisp. Madame Raquin displayed a more unbending, a more gossipy disposition, and, to tell the truth, it was she who attracted and retained the customers.

For three years, days followed days and resembled one another. Camille did not once absent himself from his office. His mother and wife hardly ever left the shop. Therese, residing in damp obscurity, in gloomy, crushing silence, saw life expand before her in all its nakedness, each night bringing the same cold couch, and each morn the same empty day.

CHAPTER IV

One day out of seven, on the Thursday evening, the Raquin family received their friends. They lit a large lamp in the dining-room, and put water on the fire to make tea. There was quite a set out. This particular evening emerged in bold relief from the others. It had become one of the customs of the family, who regarded it in the light of a middle-class orgie full of giddy gaiety. They did not retire to rest until eleven o'clock at night.

At Paris Madame Raquin had found one of her old friends, the commissary of police Michaud, who had held a post at Vernon for twenty years, lodging in the same house as the mercer. A narrow intimacy had thus been established between them; then, when the widow had sold her business to go and reside in the house beside the river, they had little by little lost sight of one another. Michaud left the provinces a few months later, and came to live peacefully in Paris, Rue de Seine, on his pension of 1,500 francs. One rainy day, he met his old friend in the Arcade of the Pont Neuf, and the same evening dined with the family.

The Thursday receptions began in this way: the former commissary of police got into the habit of calling on the Raquins regularly once a week. After a while he came accompanied by his son Olivier, a great fellow of thirty, dry and thin, who had married a very little woman, slow and sickly. This Olivier held the post of head clerk in the section of order and security at the Prefecture of Police, worth 3,000 francs a year, which made Camille feel particularly jealous. From the first day he made his appearance, Therese detested this cold, rigid individual, who imagined he honoured the shop in the arcade by making a display of his great shrivelled-up frame, and the exhausted condition of his poor little wife.

Camille introduced another guest, an old clerk at the Orleans Railway, named Grivet, who had been twenty years in the service of the company, where he now held the position of head clerk, and earned 2,100 francs a year. It was he who gave out the work in the office where Camille had found employment, and the latter showed him certain respect. Camille, in his day dreams, had said to himself that Grivet would one day die, and that he would perhaps take his place at the end of a decade or so. Grivet was delighted at the welcome Madame Raquin gave him, and he returned every week with perfect regularity. Six months later, his Thursday visit had become, in his way of thinking, a duty: he went to the Arcade of the Pont Neuf, just as he went every morning to his office, that is to say mechanically, and with the instinct of a brute.

From this moment, the gatherings became charming. At seven o'clock Madame Raquin lit the fire, set the lamp in the centre of the table, placed a box of dominoes beside it, and wiped the tea service which was in the sideboard. Precisely at eight o'clock old Michaud and Grivet met before the shop, one coming from the Rue de Seine, and the other from the Rue Mazarine. As soon as they entered, all the family went up to the first floor. There, in the dining-room, they seated themselves round the table waiting for Olivier Michaud and his wife who always arrived late. When the party was complete, Madame Raquin poured out the tea. Camille emptied the box of dominoes on the oilcloth table cover, and everyone became deeply interested in their hands. Henceforth nothing could be heard but the jingle of dominoes. At the end of each game, the players quarrelled for two or three minutes, then mournful silence was resumed, broken by the sharp clanks of the dominoes.

Therese played with an indifference that irritated Camille. She took Francois, the great tabby cat that Madame Raquin had brought from Vernon, on her lap, caressing it with one hand, whilst she placed her dominoes with the other. These Thursday evenings were a torture to her. Frequently she complained of being unwell, of a bad headache, so as not to play, and remain there doing nothing, and half asleep. An elbow on the table, her cheek resting on the palm of her hand, she watched the guests of her aunt and husband through a sort of yellow, smoky mist coming from the lamp. All these faces exasperated her. She looked from one to the other in profound disgust and secret irritation.

Old Michaud exhibited a pasty countenance, spotted with red blotches, one of those death-like faces of an old man fallen into second childhood; Grivet had the narrow visage, the round eyes, the thin lips of an idiot. Olivier, whose bones were piercing his cheeks, gravely carried a stiff, insignificant head on a ridiculous body; as to Suzanne, the wife of Olivier, she was quite pale, with expressionless eyes, white lips, and a soft face. And Therese could not find one human being, not one living being among these grotesque and sinister creatures, with whom she was shut up; sometimes she had hallucinations, she imagined herself buried at the bottom of a tomb, in company with mechanical corpses, who, when the strings were pulled, moved their heads, and agitated their legs and arms. The thick atmosphere of the dining-room stifled her; the shivering silence, the yellow gleams of the lamp penetrated her with vague terror, and inexpressible anguish.

Below, to the door of the shop, they had fixed a bell whose sharp tinkle announced the entrance of customers. Therese had her ear on the alert; and when the bell rang, she rapidly ran downstairs quite relieved, delighted at being able to quit the dining-room. She slowly served the purchaser, and when she found herself alone, she sat down behind the counter where she remained as long as possible, dreading going upstairs again, and in the enjoyment of real pleasure at no longer having Grivet and Olivier before her eyes. The damp air of the shop calmed the burning fever of her hands, and she again fell into the customary grave reverie.

But she could not remain like this for long. Camille became angry at her absence. He failed to comprehend how anyone could prefer the shop to the dining-room on a Thursday evening, and he leant over the banister, to look for his wife.

"What's the matter?" he would shout. "What are you doing there? Why don't you come up? Grivet has the devil's own luck. He has just won again."

The young woman rose painfully, and ascending to the dining-room resumed her seat opposite old Michaud, whose pendent lips gave heartrending smiles. And, until eleven o'clock, she remained oppressed in her chair, watching Francois whom she held in her arms, so as to avoid seeing the cardboard dolls grimacing around her.

CHAPTER V

One Thursday, Camille, on returning from his office, brought with him a great fellow with square shoulders, whom he pushed in a familiar manner into the shop.

"Mother," he said to Madame Raquin, pointing to the newcomer, "do you recognise this gentleman?"

The old mercer looked at the strapping blade, seeking among her recollections and finding nothing, while Therese placidly observed the scene.

"What!" resumed Camille, "you don't recognise Laurent, little Laurent, the son of daddy Laurent who owns those beautiful fields of corn out Jeufosse way. Don't you remember? I went to school with him; he came to fetch me of a morning on leaving the house of his uncle, who was our neighbour, and you used to give him slices of bread and jam."

All at once Madame Raquin recollected little Laurent, whom she found very much grown. It was quite ten years since she had seen him. She now did her best to make him forget her lapse of memory in greeting him, by recalling a thousand little incidents of the past, and by adopting a wheedling manner towards him that was quite maternal. Laurent had seated himself. With a peaceful smile on his lips, he replied to the questions addressed to him in a clear voice, casting calm and easy glances around him.

"Just imagine," said Camille, "this joker has been employed at the Orleans-Railway-Station for eighteen months, and it was only to-night that we met and recognised one another—the administration is so vast, so important!"

As the young man made this remark, he opened his eyes wider, and pinched his lips, proud to be a humble wheel in such a large machine. Shaking his head, he continued:

"Oh! but he is in a good position. He has studied. He already earns 1,500 francs a year. His father sent him to college. He had read for the bar, and learnt painting. That is so, is it not, Laurent? You'll dine with us?"

"I am quite willing," boldly replied the other.

He got rid of his hat and made himself comfortable in the shop, while Madame Raquin ran off to her stewpots. Therese, who had not yet pronounced a word, looked at the new arrival. She had never seen such a man before. Laurent, who was tall and robust, with a florid complexion, astonished her. It was with a feeling akin to admiration, that she contemplated his low forehead planted with coarse black hair, his full cheeks, his red lips, his regular features of sanguineous beauty. For an instant her eyes rested on his neck, a neck that was thick and short, fat and powerful. Then she became lost in the contemplation of his great hands which he kept spread out on his knees: the fingers were square; the clenched fist must be enormous and would fell an ox.

Laurent was a real son of a peasant, rather heavy in gait, with an arched back, with movements that were slow and precise, and an obstinate tranquil manner. One felt that his apparel concealed round and well-developed muscles, and a body of thick hard flesh. Therese examined him with curiosity, glancing from his fists to his face, and experienced little shivers when her eyes fell on his bull-like neck.

Camille spread out his Buffon volumes, and his serials at 10 centimes the number, to show his friend that he also studied. Then, as if answering an inquiry he had been making of himself for some minutes, he said to Laurent:

"But, surely you must know my wife? Don't you remember that little cousin who used to play with us at Vernon?"

"I had no difficulty in recognising Madame," answered Laurent, looking Therese full in the face.

This penetrating glance troubled the young woman, who, nevertheless, gave a forced smile, and after exchanging a few words with Laurent and her husband, hurried away to join her aunt, feeling ill at ease.

As soon as they had seated themselves at table, and commenced the soup, Camille thought it right to be attentive to his friend.

"How is your father?" he inquired.

"Well, I don't know," answered Laurent. "We are not on good terms; we ceased corresponding five years ago."

"Bah!" exclaimed the clerk, astonished at such a monstrosity.

"Yes," continued the other, "the dear man has ideas of his own. As he is always at law with his neighbours, he sent me to college, in the fond hope that later on, he would find in me an advocate who would win him all his actions. Oh! daddy Laurent has naught but useful ambitions; he even wants to get something out of his follies."

"And you wouldn't be an advocate?" inquired Camille, more and more astonished.

"Faith, no," answered his friend with a smile. "For a couple of years I pretended to follow the classes, so as to draw the allowance of 1,200 francs which my father made me. I lived with one of my college chums, who is a painter, and I set about painting also. It amused me. The calling is droll, and not at all fatiguing. We smoked and joked all the live-long day."

The Raquin family opened their eyes in amazement.

"Unfortunately," continued Laurent, "this could not last. My father found out that I was telling him falsehoods. He stopped my 100 francs a month, and invited me to return and plough the land with him. I then tried to paint pictures on religious subjects which proved bad business. As I could plainly see that I was going to die of hunger, I sent art to the deuce and sought employment. My father will die one of these days, and I am waiting for that event to live and do nothing."

Laurent spoke in a tranquil tone. In a few words he had just related a characteristic tale that depicted him at full length. In reality he was an idle fellow, with the appetite of a full-blooded man for everything, and very pronounced ideas as to easy and lasting employment. The only ambition of this great powerful frame was to do nothing, to grovel in idleness and satiation from hour to hour. He wanted to eat well, sleep well, to abundantly satisfy his passions, without moving from his place, without running the risk of the slightest fatigue.

The profession of advocate had terrified him, and he shuddered at the idea of tilling the soil. He had plunged into art, hoping to find therein a calling suitable to an idle man. The paint-brush struck him as being an instrument light to handle, and he fancied success easy. His dream was a life of cheap sensuality, a beautiful existence full of houris, of repose on divans, of victuals and intoxication.

The dream lasted so long as daddy Laurent sent the crown pieces. But when the young man, who was already thirty, perceived the wolf at the door, he began to reflect. Face to face with privations, he felt himself a coward. He would not have accepted a day without bread, for the utmost glory art could bestow. As he had said himself, he sent art to the deuce, as soon as he recognised that it would never suffice to satisfy his numerous requirements. His first efforts had been below mediocrity; his peasant eyes caught a clumsy, slovenly view of nature; his muddy, badly drawn, grimacing pictures, defied all criticism.

But he did not seem to have an over-dose of vanity for an artist; he was not in dire despair when he had to put aside his brushes. All he really regretted was the vast studio of his college chum, where he had been voluptuously grovelling for four or five years. He also regretted the women who came to pose there. Nevertheless he found himself at ease in his position as clerk; he lived very well in a brutish fashion, and he was fond of this daily task, which did not fatigue him, and soothed his mind. Still one thing irritated him: the food at the eighteen sous ordinaries failed to appease the gluttonous appetite of his stomach.

As Camille listened to his friend, he contemplated him with all the astonishment of a simpleton. This feeble man was dreaming, in a childish manner, of this studio life which his friend had been alluding to, and he questioned Laurent on the subject.

"So," said he, "there were lady models who posed before you in the nude?"

"Oh! yes," answered Laurent with a smile, and looking at Therese, who had turned deadly pale.

"You must have thought that very funny," continued Camille, laughing like a child. "It would have made me feel most awkward. I expect you were quite scandalised the first time it happened."

Laurent had spread out one of his great hands and was attentively looking at the palm. His fingers gave slight twitches, and his cheeks became flushed.

"The first time," he answered, as if speaking to himself, "I fancy I thought it quite natural. This devilish art is exceedingly amusing, only it does not bring in a sou. I had a red-haired girl as model who was superb, firm white flesh, gorgeous bust, hips as wide as . . . "

Laurent, raising his head, saw Therese mute and motionless opposite, gazing at him with ardent fixedness. Her dull black eyes seemed like two fathomless holes, and through her parted lips could be perceived the rosy tint of the inside of her mouth. She seemed as if overpowered by what she heard, and lost in thought. She continued listening.

Laurent looked from Therese to Camille, and the former painter restrained a smile. He completed his phrase by a broad voluptuous gesture, which the young woman followed with her eyes. They were at dessert, and Madame Raquin had just run downstairs to serve a customer.

When the cloth was removed Laurent, who for some minutes had been thoughtful, turned to Camille.

"You know," he blurted out, "I must paint your portrait."

This idea delighted Madame Raquin and her son, but Therese remained silent.

"It is summer-time," resumed Laurent, "and as we leave the office at four o'clock, I can come here, and let you give me a sitting for a couple of hours in the evening. The picture will be finished in a week."

"That will be fine," answered Camille, flushed with joy. "You shall dine with us. I will have my hair curled, and put on my black frock coat."

Eight o'clock struck. Grivet and Michaud made their entry. Olivier and Suzanne arrived behind them.

When Camille introduced his friend to the company, Grivet pinched his lips. He detested Laurent whose salary, according to his idea, had risen far too rapidly. Besides, the introduction of a new-comer was quite an important matter, and the guests of the Raquins could not receive an individual unknown to them, without some display of coldness.

Laurent behaved very amicably. He grasped the situation, and did his best to please the company, so as to make himself acceptable to them at once. He related anecdotes, enlivened the party by his merry laughter, and even won the friendship of Grivet.

That evening Therese made no attempt to go down to the shop. She remained seated on her chair until eleven o'clock, playing and talking, avoiding the eyes of Laurent, who for that matter did not trouble himself about her. The sanguineous temperament of this strapping fellow, his full voice and jovial laughter, troubled the young woman and threw her into a sort of nervous anguish.

CHAPTER VI

Henceforth, Laurent called almost every evening on the Raquins. He lived in the Rue Saint-Victor, opposite the Port aux Vins, where he rented a small furnished room at 18 francs a month. This attic, pierced at the top by a lift-up window, measured barely nine square yards, and Laurent was in the habit of going home as late as possible at night. Previous to his meeting with Camille, the state of his purse not permitting him to idle away his time in the cafes, he loitered at the cheap eating-houses where he took his dinner, smoking his pipe and sipping his coffee and brandy which cost him three sous. Then he slowly gained the Rue Saint-Victor, sauntering along the quays, where he seated himself on the benches, in mild weather.

The shop in the Arcade of the Pont Neuf became a charming retreat, warm and quiet, where he found amicable conversation and attention. He saved the three sous his coffee and brandy cost him, and gluttonously swallowed the excellent tea prepared by Madame Raquin. He remained there until ten o'clock, dozing and digesting as if he were at home; and before taking his departure, assisted Camille to put up the shutters and close the shop for the night.

One evening, he came with his easel and box of colours. He was to commence the portrait of Camille on the morrow. A canvas was purchased, minute preparations made, and the artist at last took the work in hand in the room occupied by the married couple, where Laurent said the light was the best.

He took three evenings to draw the head. He carefully trailed the charcoal over the canvas with short, sorry strokes, his rigid, cold drawing recalling in a grotesque fashion that of the primitive masters. He copied the face of Camille with a hesitating hand, as a pupil copies an academical figure, with a clumsy exactitude that conveyed a scowl to the face. On the fourth day, he placed tiny little dabs of colour on his palette, and commenced painting with the point of the brush; he then dotted the canvas with small dirty spots, and made short strokes altogether as if he had been using a pencil.

At the end of each sitting, Madame Raquin and Camille were in ecstasies. But Laurent said they must wait, that the resemblance would soon come.

Since the portrait had been commenced, Therese no longer quitted the room, which had been transformed into a studio. Leaving her aunt alone behind the counter, she ran upstairs at the least pretext, and forgot herself watching Laurent paint.

Still grave and oppressed, paler and more silent, she sat down and observed the labour of the brushes. But this sight did not seem to amuse her very much. She came to the spot, as though attracted by some power, and she remained, as if riveted there. Laurent at times turned round, with a smile, inquiring whether the portrait pleased her. But she barely answered, a shiver ran through her frame, and she resumed her meditative trance.

Laurent, returning at night to the Rue Saint-Victor, reasoned with himself at length, discussing in his mind, whether he should become the lover of Therese, or not.

"Here is a little woman," said he to himself, "who will be my sweetheart whenever I choose. She is always there, behind my back, examining, measuring me, summing me up. She trembles. She has a strange face that is mute and yet impassioned. What a miserable creature that Camille is, to be sure."

And Laurent inwardly laughed as he thought of his pale, thin friend. Then he resumed:

"She is bored to death in that shop. I go there, because I have nowhere else to go to, otherwise they would not often catch me in the Arcade of the Pont Neuf. It is damp and sad. A woman must be wearied to death there. I please her, I am sure of it; then, why not me rather than another?"

He stopped. Self-conceit was getting the better of him. Absorbed in thought, he watched the Seine running by.

"Anyhow, come what may," he exclaimed, "I shall kiss her at the first opportunity. I bet she falls at once into my arms."

As he resumed his walk, he was seized with indecision.

"But she is ugly," thought he. "She has a long nose, and a big mouth. Besides, I have not the least love for her. I shall perhaps get myself into trouble. The matter requires reflection."

Laurent, who was very prudent, turned these thoughts over in his head for a whole week. He calculated all the possible inconveniences of an intrigue with Therese, and only decided to attempt the adventure, when he felt convinced that it could be attended by no evil consequences. Therese would have every interest to conceal their intimacy, and he could get rid of her whenever he pleased. Even admitting that Camille discovered everything, and got angry, he would knock him down, if he became spiteful. From every point of view that matter appeared to Laurent easy and engaging.

Henceforth he enjoyed gentle quietude, waiting for the hour to strike. He had made up his mind to act boldly at the first opportunity. In the future he saw comfortable evenings, with all the Raquins contributing to his enjoyment: Therese giving him her love, Madame Raquin wheedling him like a mother, and Camille chatting with him so that he might not feel too dull, at night, in the shop.

The portrait was almost completed, but the opportunity he desired did not occur. Therese, depressed and anxious, continued to remain in the room. But so did Camille, and Laurent was in despair at being unable to get rid of him. Nevertheless, the time came when he found himself obliged to mention that the portrait would be finished on the morrow, and Madame Raquin thereupon announced that they would celebrate the completion of the work of the artist by dining together.

The next day, when Laurent had given the canvas the last touch, all the family assembled to go into raptures over the striking resemblance. The portrait was vile, a dirty grey colour with large violescent patches. Laurent could not use even the brightest colours, without making them dull and muddy. In spite of himself he had exaggerated the wan complexion of his model, and the countenance of Camille resembled the greenish visage of a person who had met death by drowning. The grimacing drawing threw the features into convulsions, thus rendering the sinister resemblance all the more striking. But Camille was delighted; he declared that he had the appearance of a person of distinction on the canvas.

When he had thoroughly admired his own face, he declared he would go and fetch a couple of bottles of champagne. Madame Raquin went down to the shop, and the artist was alone with Therese.

The young woman had remained seated, gazing vaguely in front of her. Laurent hesitated. He examined the portrait, and played with his brushes. There was not much time to lose. Camille might come back, and the opportunity would perhaps not occur again. The painter abruptly turned round, and found himself face to face with Therese.

They contemplated one another for a few seconds. Then, with a violent movement, Laurent bent down, and pressed the young woman to him. Throwing back her head he crushed her mouth beneath his lips. She made a savage, angry effort at revolt, and, then all at once gave in. They exchanged not a word. The act was silent and brutal.

CHAPTER VII

The two sweethearts from the commencement found their intrigue necessary, inevitable and quite natural. At their first interview they conversed familiarly, kissing one another without embarrassment, and without a blush, as if their intimacy had dated back several years. They lived quite at ease in their new situation, with a tranquillity and an independence that were perfect.

They made their appointments. Therese being unable to go out, it was arranged that Laurent should come to see her. In a clear, firm voice the young woman explained to him the plan she had conceived. The interview would take place in the nuptial chamber. The sweetheart would pass by the passage which ran into the arcade, and Therese would open the door on the staircase to him. During this time, Camille would be at his office, and Madame Raquin below, in the shop. This was a daring arrangement that ought to succeed.

Laurent accepted. There was a sort of brutal temerity in his prudence, the temerity of a man with big fists. Choosing a pretext, he obtained permission from his chief to absent himself for a couple of hours, and hastened to the Arcade of the Pont Neuf.

The dealer in imitation jewelry was seated just opposite the door of the passage, and he had to wait until she was busy, until some young work-girl came to purchase a ring or a brooch made of brass. Then, rapidly entering the passage, he ascended the narrow, dark staircase, leaning against the walls which were clammy with damp. He stumbled against the stone steps, and each time he did so, he felt a red-hot iron piercing his chest. A door opened, and on the threshold, in the midst of a gleam of white light he perceived Therese, who closing the door after him, threw her arms about his neck.

Laurent was astonished to find his sweetheart handsome. He had never seen her before as she appeared to him then. Therese, supple and strong, pressed him in her arms, flinging her head backward, while on her visage coursed ardent rays of light and passionate smiles. This face seemed as if transfigured, with its moist lips and sparkling eyes. It now had a fond caressing look. It radiated. She was beautiful with the strong beauty born of passionate abandon.

When Laurent parted from her, after his initial visit, he staggered like a drunken man, and the next day, on recovering his cunning prudent calm, he asked himself whether he should return to this young woman whose kisses gave him the fever. First of all he positively decided to keep to himself. Then he had a cowardly feeling. He sought to forget, to avoid seeing Therese, and yet she always seemed to be there, implacably extending her arms. The physical suffering that this spectacle caused him became intolerable.

He gave way. He arranged another meeting, and returned to the Arcade of the Pont Neuf.

From that day forth, Therese entered into his life. He did not yet accept her, although he bore with her. He had his hours of terror, his moments of prudence, and, altogether this intrigue caused him disagreeable agitation. But his discomfort and his fears disappeared. The meetings continued and multiplied.

Therese experienced no hesitation. She went straight where her passion urged her to go. This woman whom circumstances had bowed down, and who had at length drawn herself up erect, now revealed all her being and explained her life.

"Oh! if you only knew," said she, "how I have suffered. I was brought up in the tepid damp room of an invalid. I slept in the same bed as Camille. At night I got as far away from him as I could, to avoid the sickly odour of his body. He was naughty and obstinate. He would not take his physic unless I shared it with him. To please my aunt I was obliged to swallow a dose of every drug. I don't know how it is I have survived. They made me ugly. They robbed me of the only thing I possessed, and it is impossible for you to love me as I love you."

She broke off and wept, and after kissing Laurent, continued with bitter hatred:

"I do not wish them any harm. They brought me up, they received me, and shielded me from misery. But I should have preferred abandonment to their hospitality. I had a burning desire for the open air. When quite young, my dream was to rove barefooted along the dusty roads, holding out my hand for charity, living like a gipsy. I have been told that my mother was a daughter of the chief of a tribe in Africa. I have often thought of her, and I understood that I belonged to her by blood and instinct. I should have liked to have never parted from her, and to have crossed the sand slung at her back.

"Ah! what a childhood! I still feel disgust and rebellion, when I recall the long days I passed in the room where Camille was at death's door. I sat bent over the fire, stupidly watching the infusions simmer, and feeling my limbs growing stiff. And I could not move. My aunt scolded me if I made a noise. Later on, I tasted profound joy in the little house beside the river; but I was already half feeble, I could barely walk, and when I tried to run I fell down. Then they buried me alive in this vile shop."

After a pause, she resumed:

"You will hardly credit how bad they have made me. They have turned me into a liar and a hypocrite. They have stifled me with their middle-class gentleness, and I can hardly understand how it is that there is still blood in my veins. I have lowered my eyes, and given myself a mournful, idiotic face like theirs. I have led their deathlike life. When you saw me I looked like a blockhead, did I not? I was grave, overwhelmed, brutalised. I no longer had any hope. I thought of flinging myself into the Seine.

"But previous to this depression, what nights of anger I had. Down there at Vernon, in my frigid room, I bit my pillow to stifle my cries. I beat myself, taxed myself with cowardice. My blood was on the boil, and I would have lacerated my body. On two occasions, I wanted to run away, to go straight before me, towards the sun; but my courage failed. They had turned me into a docile brute with their tame benevolence and sickly tenderness. Then I lied, I always lied. I remained there quite gentle, quite silent, dreaming of striking and biting."

After a silence, she continued:

"I do not know why I consented to marry Camille. I did not protest, from a feeling of a sort of disdainful indifference. I pitied the child. When I played with him, I felt my fingers sink into the flesh of his limbs as into damp clay. I took him because my aunt offered him to me, and because I never intended to place any restraint on my actions on his account.

"I found my husband just the same little suffering boy whose bed I had shared when I was six years old. He was just as frail, just as plaintive, and he still had that insipid odour of a sick child that had been so repugnant to me previously. I am relating all this so that you may not be jealous. I was seized with a sort of disgust. I remembered the physic I had drank. I got as far away from him as the bed would allow, and I passed terrible nights. But you, you—"

Therese drew herself up, bending backward, her fingers imprisoned in the massive hands of Laurent, gazing at his broad shoulders, and enormous neck.

"You, I love you," she continued. "I loved you from the day Camille pushed you into the shop. You have perhaps no esteem for me, because I gave way at once. Truly, I know not how it happened. I am proud. I am passionate. I would have liked to have beaten you, the first day, when you kissed me. I do not know how it was I loved you; I hated you rather. The sight of you irritated me, and made me suffer. When you were there, my nerves were strained fit to snap. My head became quite empty. I was ready to commit a crime.

"Oh! how I suffered! And I sought this suffering. I waited for you to arrive. I loitered round your chair, so as to move in your breath, to drag my clothes over yours. It seemed as though your blood cast puffs of heat on me as I passed, and it was this sort of burning cloud in which you were enveloped, that attracted me, and detained me beside you in spite of my secret revolt. You remember when you were painting here: a fatal power attracted me to your side, and I breathed your air with cruel delight. I know I seemed to be begging for kisses, I felt ashamed of my bondage, I felt I should fall, if you were to touch me. But I gave way to my cowardice, I shivered with cold, waiting until you chose to take me in your arms."

When Therese ceased speaking, she was quivering, as though proud at being avenged. In this bare and chilly room were enacted scenes of burning lust, sinister in their brutality.

On her part Therese seemed to revel in daring. The only precaution she would take when expecting her lover was to tell her aunt she was going upstairs to rest. But then, when he was there she never bothered about avoiding noise, walking about and talking. At first this terrified Laurent.

"For God's sake," he whispered, "don't make so much noise. Madame Raquin will hear."

Therese would laugh. "Who cares, you are always so worried. She is at her counter and won't leave. She is too afraid of being robbed. Besides, you can hide."

Laurent's passion had not yet stifled his native peasant caution, but soon he grew used to the risks of these meetings, only a few yards from the old woman.

One day, fearing her niece was ill, Madame Raquin climbed the stairs.

Therese never bothered to bolt the bedroom door.

At the sound of the woman's heavy step on the wooden stairs, Laurent became frantic. Therese laughed as she saw him searching for his waistcoat and hat. She grabbed his arm and pushed him down at the foot of the bed. With perfect self-possession she whispered:

"Stay there. Don't move."

She threw all his clothes that were lying about over him and covered them with a white petticoat she had taken off. Without losing her calm, she lay down, half-naked, with her hair loose.

When Madame Raquin quietly opened the door and tiptoed to the bed the younger woman pretended to be asleep. Laurent, under all the clothes was in a panic.

"Therese," asked the old lady with some concern, "are you all right, my dear?"

Therese, opening her eyes and yawning, answered that she had a terrible migraine. She begged her aunt to let her sleep some more. The old lady left the room as quietly as she had entered it.

"So you see," Therese said triumphantly, "there is no reason to worry. These people are not in love. They are blind."

At other times Therese seemed quite mad, wandering in her mind. She would see the cat, sitting motionless and dignified, looking at them. "Look at Francois," she said to Laurent. "You'd think he understands and is planning to tell Camille everything to-night. He knows a thing or two about us. Wouldn't it be funny if one day, in the shop, he just started talking."

This idea was delightful to Therese but Laurent felt a shudder run through him as he looked at the cat's big green eyes. Therese's hold on him was not total and he was scared. He got up and put the cat out of the room.

CHAPTER VIII

Laurent was perfectly happy of an evening, in the shop. He generally returned from the office with Camille. Madame Raquin had formed quite a motherly affection for him. She knew he was short of cash, and indifferently nourished, that he slept in a garret; and she had told him, once for all, that a seat would always be kept for him at their table. She liked this young fellow with that expansive feeling that old women display for people who come from their own part of the country, bringing with them memories of the past.

The young man took full advantage of this hospitality. Before going to dinner, after leaving the office for the night, he and Camille went for a stroll on the quays. Both found satisfaction in this intimacy. They dawdled along, chatting with one another, which prevented them feeling dull, and after a time decided to go and taste the soup prepared by Madame Raquin. Laurent opened the shop door as if he were master of the house, seated himself astride a chair, smoking and expectorating as though at home.

The presence of Therese did not embarrass him in the least. He treated the young woman with friendly familiarity, paying her commonplace compliments without a line of his face becoming disturbed. Camille laughed, and, as his wife confined herself to answering his friend in monosyllables, he firmly believed they detested one another. One day he even reproached Therese with what he termed her coldness for Laurent.

Laurent had made a correct guess: he had become the sweetheart of the woman, the friend of the husband, the spoilt child of the mother. Never had he enjoyed such a capital time. His position in the family struck him as quite natural. He was on the most friendly terms with Camille, in regard to whom he felt neither anger nor remorse. He was so sure of being prudent and calm that he did not even keep watch on his gestures and speech. The egotism he displayed in the enjoyment of his good fortune, shielded him from any fault. All that kept him from kissing Therese in the shop was the fear that he would not be allowed to come any more. He would not have cared a bit about hurting Camille and his mother.

Therese, who was of a more nervous and quivering temperament, was compelled to play a part, and she played it to perfection, thanks to the clever hypocrisy she had acquired in her bringing up. For nearly fifteen years, she had been lying, stifling her fever, exerting an implacable will to appear gloomy and half asleep. It cost her nothing to keep this mask on her face, which gave her an appearance of icy frigidity.

When Laurent entered the shop, he found her glum, her nose longer, her lips thinner. She was ugly, cross, unapproachable. Nevertheless, she did not exaggerate her effects, but only played her former part, without awakening attention by greater harshness. She experienced extraordinary pleasure in deceiving Camille and Madame Raquin. She was aware she was doing wrong, and at times she felt a ferocious desire to rise from table and smother Laurent with kisses, just to show her husband and aunt that she was not a fool, and that she had a sweetheart.

At moments, she felt giddy with joy; good actress as she proved herself, she could not on such occasions refrain from singing, when her sweetheart did not happen to be there, and she had no fear of betraying herself. These sudden outbursts of gaiety charmed Madame Raquin, who taxed her niece with being too serious. The young woman, moreover, decked the window of her room with pots of flowers, and then had new paper hung in the apartment. After this she wanted a carpet, curtains and rosewood furniture.

The nature of the circumstances seemed to have made this woman for this man, and to have thrust one towards the other. The two together, the woman nervous and hypocritical, the man sanguineous and leading the life of a brute, formed a powerful couple allied. The one completed the other, and they mutually protected themselves. At night, at table, in the pale light of the lamp, one felt the strength of their union, at the sight of the heavy, smiling face of Laurent, opposite the mute, impenetrable mask of Therese.

Those evenings were pleasant and calm. In the silence, in the transparent shadow and cool atmosphere, arose friendly conversation. The family and their guest sat close together round the table. After the dessert, they chatted about a thousand trifles of the day, about incidents that had occurred the day before, about their hopes for the morrow.

Camille liked Laurent, as much as he was capable of liking anybody, after the fashion of a contented egotist, and Laurent seemed to show him equal attachment. Between them there was an exchange of kind sentences, of obliging gestures, and thoughtful attentions. Madame Raquin, with placid countenance, contributed her peacefulness to the tranquillity of the scene, which resembled a gathering of old friends who knew one another to the heart, and who confidently relied on the faith of their friendship.

Therese, motionless, peaceful like the others, observed this joy, this smiling depression of these people of the middle class, and in her heart there was savage laughter; all her being jeered, but her face maintained its frigid rigidity. Ah! how she deceived these worthy people, and how delighted she was to deceive them with such triumphant impudence. Her sweetheart, at this moment, was like a person unknown to her, a comrade of her husband, a sort of simpleton and interloper concerning whom she had no need to concern herself. This atrocious comedy, these duperies of life, this comparison between the burning kisses in the daytime, and the indifference played at night, gave new warmth to the blood of the young woman.

When by chance Madame Raquin and Camille went downstairs, Therese bounded from her chair, to silently, and with brutal energy, press her lips to those of her sweetheart, remaining thus breathless and choking until she heard the stairs creak. Then, she briskly seated herself again, and resumed her glum grimace, while Laurent calmly continued the interrupted conversation with Camille. It was like a rapid, blinding flash of lightning in a leaden sky.

On Thursday, the evening became a little more animated. Laurent, although bored to death, nevertheless made a point of not missing one of these gatherings. As a measure of prudence he desired to be known and esteemed by the friends of Camille. So he had to lend an ear to the idle talk of Grivet and old Michaud. The latter always related the same tales of robbery and murder, while Grivet spoke at the same time about his clerks, his chiefs, and his administration, until the young man sought refuge beside Olivier and Suzanne, whose stupidity seemed less wearisome. But he soon asked for the dominoes.

It was on Thursday evening that Laurent and Therese arranged the day and hour of their meeting. In the bustle attending the departure, when Madame Raquin and Camille accompanied the guest to the door of the arcade, the young woman approached Laurent, to whom she spoke in an undertone, as she pressed his hand. At times, when all had turned their backs, she kissed him, out of a sort of bravado.

The life of shocks and appeasements, lasted eight months. The sweethearts lived in complete beatitude; Therese no longer felt dull, and was perfectly contented. Laurent satiated, pampered, fatter than before, had but one fear, that of seeing this delightful existence come to an end.

CHAPTER IX

One afternoon, as Laurent was leaving his office to run and meet Therese who was expecting him, his chief gave him to understand that in future he was forbidden to absent himself. He had taken too many holidays already, and the authorities had decided to dismiss him if he again went out in office hours.

Riveted to his chair, he remained in despair until eventide. He had to earn his living, and dared not lose his place. At night the wrathful countenance of Therese was a torture to him, and he was unable to find an opportunity to explain to her how it was he had broken his word. At length, as Camille was putting up the shutters, he briskly approached the young woman, to murmur in an undertone:

"We shall be unable to see one another any more. My chief refuses to give me permission to go out."

Camille came into the shop, and Laurent was obliged to withdraw without giving any further information, leaving Therese under the disagreeable influence of this abrupt and unpleasant announcement. Exasperated at anyone daring to interfere with her delectation, she passed a sleepless night, arranging extravagant plans for a meeting with her sweetheart. The following Thursday, she spoke with Laurent for a minute at the most. Their anxiety was all the keener as they did not know where to meet for the purpose of consulting and coming to an understanding. The young woman, on this occasion, gave her sweetheart another appointment which for the second time he failed to keep, and she then had but one fixed idea—to see him at any cost.

For a fortnight Laurent was unable to speak to Therese alone, and he then felt how necessary this woman had become to his existence. Far from experiencing any uneasiness, as formerly, at the kisses which his ladylove showered on him, he now sought her embraces with the obstinacy of a famished animal. A sanguineous passion had lurked in his muscles, and now that his sweetheart was taken from him, this passion burst out in blind violence. He was madly in love. This thriving brutish nature seemed unconscious in everything. He obeyed his instincts, permitting the will of his organism to lead him.

A year before, he would have burst into laughter, had he been told he would become the slave of a woman, to the point of risking his tranquillity. The hidden forces of lust that had brought about this result had been secretly proceeding within him, to end by casting him, bound hand and foot, into the arms of Therese. At this hour, he was in dread lest he should omit to be prudent. He no longer dared go of an evening to the shop in the Arcade of the Pont Neuf lest he should commit some folly. He no longer belonged to himself. His ladylove, with her feline suppleness, her nervous flexibility, had glided, little by little, into each fibre of his body. This woman was as necessary to his life as eating and drinking.

He would certainly have committed some folly, had he not received a letter from Therese, asking him to remain at home the following evening. His sweetheart promised him to call about eight o'clock.

On quitting the office, he got rid of Camille by saying he was tired, and should go to bed at once. Therese, after dinner, also played her part. She mentioned a customer who had moved without paying her, and acting the indignant creditor who would listen to nothing, declared that she intended calling on her debtor with the view of asking for payment of the money that was due. The customer now lived at Batignolles. Madame Raquin and Camille considered this a long way to go, and thought it doubtful whether the journey would have a satisfactory result; but they expressed no surprise, and allowed Therese to set out on her errand in all tranquillity.

The young woman ran to the Port aux Vins, gliding over the slippery pavement, and knocking up against the passers-by, in her hurry to reach her destination. Beads of perspiration covered her face, and her hands were burning. Anyone might have taken her for a drunken woman. She rapidly ascended the staircase of the hotel, and on reaching the sixth floor, out of breath, and with wandering eyes, she perceived Laurent, who was leaning over the banister awaiting her.

She entered the garret, which was so small that she could barely turn round in it, and tearing off her hat with one hand leant against the bedstead in a faint. Through the lift-up window in the roof, which was wide open, the freshness of the evening fell upon the burning couch.

The couple remained some time in this wretched little room, as though at the bottom of a hole. All at once, Therese heard a clock in the neighbourhood strike ten. She felt as if she would have liked to have been deaf. Nevertheless, she looked for her hat which she fastened to her hair with a long pin, and then seating herself, slowly murmured:

"I must go."

Laurent fell on his knees before her, and took her hands.

"Good-bye, till we see each other again," said she, without moving.

"No, not till we see each other again!" he exclaimed, "that is too indefinite. When will you come again?"

She looked him full in the face.

"Do you wish me to be frank with you?" she inquired. "Well, then, to tell you the truth, I think I shall come no more. I have no pretext, and I cannot invent one."

"Then we must say farewell," he remarked.

"No, I will not do that!" she answered.

She pronounced these words in terrified anger. Then she added more gently, without knowing what she was saying, and without moving from her chair:

"I am going."

Laurent reflected. He was thinking of Camille.

"I wish him no harm," said he at length, without pronouncing the name: "but really he is too much in our way. Couldn't you get rid of him, send him on a journey somewhere, a long way off?"

"Ah! yes, send him on a journey!" resumed the young woman, nodding her head. "And do you imagine a man like that would consent to travel? There is only one journey, that from which you never return. But he will bury us all. People who are at their last breath, never die."

Then came a silence which was broken by Laurent who remarked:

"I had a day dream. Camille met with an accident and died, and I became your husband. Do you understand?"

"Yes, yes," answered Therese, shuddering.

Then, abruptly bending over the face of Laurent, she smothered it with kisses, and bursting into sobs, uttered these disjoined sentences amidst her tears:

"Don't talk like that, for if you do, I shall lack the strength to leave you. I shall remain here. Give me courage rather. Tell me we shall see one another again. You have need of me, have you not? Well, one of these days we shall find a way to live together."

"Then come back, come back to-morrow," said Laurent.

"But I cannot return," she answered. "I have told you. I have no pretext."

She wrung her hands and continued:

"Oh! I do not fear the scandal. If you like, when I get back, I will tell

Camille you are my sweetheart, and return here. I am trembling for you. I do not wish to disturb your life. I want to make you happy."

The prudent instincts of the young man were awakened.

"You are right," said he. "We must not behave like children. Ah! if your husband were to die!"

"If my husband were to die," slowly repeated Therese.

"We would marry," he continued, "and have nothing more to fear. What a nice, gentle life it would be!"

The young woman stood up erect. Her cheeks were pale, and she looked at her sweetheart with a clouded brow, while her lips were twitching.

"Sometimes people die," she murmured at last. "Only it is dangerous for those who survive."

Laurent did not reply.

"You see," she continued, "all the methods that are known are bad."

"You misunderstood me," said he quietly. "I am not a fool, I wish to love you in peace. I was thinking that accidents happen daily, that a foot may slip, a tile may fall. You understand. In the latter event, the wind alone is guilty."

He spoke in a strange voice. Then he smiled, and added in a caressing tone:

"Never mind, keep quiet. We will love one another fondly, and live happily. As you are unable to come here, I will arrange matters. Should we remain a few months without seeing one another, do not forget me, and bear in mind that I am labouring for your felicity."

As Therese opened the door to leave, he seized her in his arms.

"You are mine, are you not?" he continued. "You swear to belong to me, at any hour, when I choose."

"Yes!" exclaimed the young woman. "I am yours, do as you please with me."

For a moment they remained locked together and mute. Then Therese tore herself roughly away, and, without turning her head, quitted the garret and went downstairs. Laurent listened to the sound of her footsteps fading away.

When he heard the last of them, he returned to his wretched room, and went to bed. The sheets were still warm. Without closing the window, he lay on his back, his arms bare, his hands open, exposed to the fresh air. And he reflected, with his eyes on the dark blue square that the window framed in the sky.

He turned the same idea over in his head until daybreak. Previous to the visit of Therese, the idea of murdering Camille had not occurred to him. He had spoken of the death of this man, urged to do so by the facts, irritated at the thought that he would be unable to meet his sweetheart any more. And it was thus that a new corner of his unconscious nature came to be revealed.

Now that he was more calm, alone in the middle of the peaceful night, he studied the murder. The idea of death, blurted out in despair between a couple of kisses, returned implacable and keen. Racked by insomnia, and unnerved by the visit of Therese, he calculated the disadvantages and the advantages of his becoming an assassin.

All his interests urged him to commit the crime. He said to himself that as his father, the Jeufosse peasant, could not make up his mind to die, he would perhaps have to remain a clerk another ten years, eating in cheap restaurants, and living in a garret. This idea exasperated him. On the other hand, if Camille were dead, he would marry Therese, he would inherit from Madame Raquin, resign his clerkship, and saunter about in the sun. Then, he took pleasure in dreaming of this life of idleness; he saw himself with nothing to do, eating and sleeping, patiently awaiting the death of his father. And when the reality arose in the middle of his dream, he ran up against Camille, and clenched his fists to knock him down.

Laurent desired Therese; he wanted her for himself alone, to have her always within reach. If he failed to make the husband disappear, the woman would escape him. She had said so: she could not return. He would have eloped with her, carried her off somewhere, but then both would die of hunger. He risked less in killing the husband. There would be no scandal. He would simply push a man away to take his place. In his brutal logic of a peasant, he found this method excellent and natural. His innate prudence even advised this rapid expedient.

He grovelled on his bed, in perspiration, flat on his stomach, with his face against the pillow, and he remained there breathless, stifling, seeing lines of fire pass along his closed eyelids. He asked himself how he would kill Camille. Then, unable to breathe any more, he turned round at a bound to resume his position on his back, and with his eyes wide open, received full in the face, the puffs of cold air from the window, seeking in the stars, in the bluish square of sky, a piece of advice about murder, a plan of assassination.

And he found nothing. As he had told his ladylove, he was neither a child nor a fool. He wanted neither a dagger nor poison. What he sought was a subtle crime, one that could be accomplished without danger; a sort of sinister suffocation, without cries and without terror, a simple disappearance. Passion might well stir him, and urge him forward; all his being imperiously insisted on prudence. He was too cowardly, too voluptuous to risk his tranquillity. If he killed, it would be for a calm and happy life.

Little by little slumber overcame him. Fatigued and appeased, he sank into a sort of gentle and uncertain torpor. As he fell asleep, he decided he would await a favourable opportunity, and his thoughts, fleeting further and further away, lulled him to rest with the murmur:

"I will kill him, I will kill him."

Five minutes later, he was at rest, breathing with serene regularity.

Therese returned home at eleven o'clock, with a burning head, and her thoughts strained, reaching the Arcade of the Pont Neuf unconscious of the road she had taken. It seemed to her that she had just come downstairs from her visit to Laurent, so full were her ears of the words she had recently heard. She found Madame Raquin and Camille anxious and attentive; but she answered their questions sharply, saying she had been on a fools' errand, and had waited an hour on the pavement for an omnibus.

When she got into bed, she found the sheets cold and damp. Her limbs, which were still burning, shuddered with repugnance. Camille soon fell asleep, and for a long time Therese watched his wan face reposing idiotically on the pillow, with his mouth wide open. Therese drew away from her husband. She felt a desire to drive her clenched fist into that mouth.

CHAPTER X

More than three weeks passed. Laurent came to the shop every evening, looking weary and unwell. A light bluish circle surrounded his eyes, and his lips were becoming pale and chapped. Otherwise, he still maintained his obtuse tranquillity, he looked Camille in the face, and showed him the same frank friendship. Madame Raquin pampered the friend of the family the more, now that she saw him giving way to a sort of low fever.

Therese had resumed her mute, glum countenance and manner. She was more motionless, more impenetrable, more peaceful than ever. She did not seem to trouble herself in the least about Laurent. She barely looked at him, rarely exchanged a word with him, treating him with perfect indifference. Madame Raquin, who in her goodness of heart, felt pained at this attitude, sometimes said to the young man:

"Do not pay attention to the manner of my niece, I know her; her face appears cold, but her heart is warm with tenderness and devotedness."

The two sweethearts had no more meetings. Since the evening in the Rue Saint-Victor they had not met alone. At night, when they found themselves face to face, placid in appearance and like strangers to one another, storms of passion and dismay passed beneath the calm flesh of their countenance. And while with Therese, there were outbursts of fury, base ideas, and cruel jeers, with Laurent there were sombre brutalities, and poignant indecisions. Neither dared search to the bottom of their beings, to the bottom of that cloudy fever that filled their brains with a sort of thick and acrid vapour.

When they could press the hands of one another behind a door, without speaking, they did so, fit to crush them, in a short rough clasp. They would have liked, mutually, to have carried off strips of their flesh clinging to their fingers. They had naught but this pressure of hands to appease their feelings. They put all their souls into them, and asked for nothing more from one another. They waited.

One Thursday evening, before sitting down to the game of dominoes, the guests of the Raquin family had a chat, as usual. A favourite subject of conversation was afforded by the experiences of old Michaud who was plied with questions respecting the strange and sinister adventures with which he must have been connected in the discharge of his former functions. Then Grivet and Camille listened to the stories of the commissary with the affrighted and gaping countenances of small children listening to "Blue Beard" or "Tom Thumb." These tales terrified and amused them.

On this particular Thursday, Michaud, who had just given an account of a horrible murder, the details of which had made his audience shudder, added as he wagged his head:

"And a great deal never comes out at all. How many crimes remain undiscovered! How many murderers escape the justice of man!"

"What!" exclaimed Grivet astonished, "you think there are foul creatures like that walking about the streets, people who have murdered and are not arrested?"

Olivier smiled with an air of disdain.

"My dear sir," he answered in his dictatorial tone, "if they are not arrested it is because no one is aware that they have committed a murder."

This reasoning did not appear to convince Grivet, and Camille came to his assistance.

"I am of the opinion of M. Grivet," said he, with silly importance. "I should like to believe that the police do their duty, and that I never brush against a murderer on the pavement."

Olivier considered this remark a personal attack.

"Certainly the police do their duty," he exclaimed in a vexed tone. "Still we cannot do what is impossible. There are wretches who have studied crime at Satan's own school; they would escape the Divinity Himself. Isn't that so, father?"

"Yes, yes," confirmed old Michaud. "Thus, while I was at Vernon—you perhaps remember the incident, Madame Raquin—a wagoner was murdered on the highway. The corpse was found cut in pieces, at the bottom of a ditch. The authorities were never able to lay hands on the culprit. He is perhaps still living at this hour. Maybe he is our neighbour, and perhaps M. Grivet will meet him on his way home."

Grivet turned pale as a sheet. He dared not look round. He fancied the murderer of the wagoner was behind him. But for that matter, he was delighted to feel afraid.

"Well, no," he faltered, hardly knowing what he said, "well, no, I cannot believe that. But I also have a story: once upon a time a servant was put in prison for stealing a silver spoon and fork belonging to her master and mistress. Two months afterwards, while a tree was being felled, the knife and fork were discovered in the nest of a magpie. It was the magpie who was the thief. The servant was released. You see that the guilty are always punished."

Grivet triumphed. Olivier sneered.

"Then, they put the magpie in prison," said he.

"That is not what M. Grivet meant to say," answered Camille, annoyed to see his chief turned into ridicule. "Mother, give us the dominoes."

While Madame Raquin went to fetch the box, the young man, addressing Michaud, continued:

"Then you admit the police are powerless, that there are murderers walking about in the sunshine?"

"Unfortunately, yes," answered the commissary.

"It is immoral," concluded Grivet.

During this conversation, Therese and Laurent had remained silent. They had not even smiled at the folly of Grivet. Both leaning with their arms on the table, looking slightly pale, and with a vague expression in their eyes, listened. At one moment those dark, ardent orbs had met. And small drops of perspiration pearled at the roots of the hair of Therese, while chilly puffs of breath gave imperceptible shivers to the skin of Laurent.

CHAPTER XI

Sometimes on a Sunday, when the weather was fine, Camille forced Therese to go out with him, for a walk in the Champs Elysees. The young woman would have preferred to remain in the damp obscurity of the arcade, for the exercise fatigued her, and it worried her to be on the arm of her husband, who dragged her along the pavement, stopping before the shop windows, expressing his astonishment, making reflections, and then falling into ridiculous spells of silence.

But Camille insisted on these Sunday outings, which gave him the satisfaction of showing off his wife. When he met a colleague, particularly one of his chiefs, he felt quite proud to exchange bows with him, in the company of Madame. Besides, he walked for the sake of walking, and he did so almost in silence, stiff and deformed in his Sunday clothes, dragging along his feet, and looking silly and vain. It made Therese suffer to be seen arm in arm with such a man.

On these walking-out days, Madame Raquin accompanied her children to the end of the arcade, where she embraced them as if they were leaving on a journey, giving them endless advice, accompanied by fervent prayers.

"Particularly, beware of accidents," she would say. "There are so many vehicles in the streets of Paris! Promise me not to get in a crowd."

At last she allowed them to set out, but she followed them a considerable distance with her eyes, before returning to the shop. Her lower limbs were becoming unwieldy which prohibited her taking long walks.

On other occasions, but more rarely, the married couple went out of Paris, as far as Saint-Ouen or Asnieres, where they treated themselves to a dish of fried fish in one of the restaurants beside the river. These were regarded as days of great revelry which were spoken of a month beforehand. Therese engaged more willingly, almost with joy, in these excursions which kept her in the open air until ten or eleven o'clock at night. Saint-Ouen, with its green isles, reminded her of Vernon, and rekindled all the wild love she had felt for the Seine when a little girl.

She seated herself on the gravel, dipped her hands in the water, feeling full of life in the burning heat of the sun, attenuated by the fresh puffs of breeze in the shade. While she tore and soiled her frock on the stones and clammy ground, Camille neatly spread out his pocket-handkerchief and sank down beside her with endless precautions. Latterly the young couple almost invariably took Laurent with them. He enlivened the excursion by his laughter and strength of a peasant.

One Sunday, Camille, Therese and Laurent left for Saint-Ouen after breakfast, at about eleven o'clock. The outing had been projected a long time, and was to be the last of the season. Autumn approached, and the cold breezes at night, began to make the air chilly.

On this particular morning, the sky maintained all its blue serenity. It proved warm in the sun and tepid in the shade. The party decided that they must take advantage of the last fine weather.

Hailing a passing cab they set out, accompanied by the pitiful expressions of uneasiness, and the anxious effusions of the old mercer. Crossing Paris, they left the vehicle at the fortifications, and gained Saint-Ouen on foot. It was noon. The dusty road, brightly lit up by the sun, had the blinding whiteness of snow. The air was intensely warm, heavy and pungent. Therese, on the arm of Camille, walked with short steps, concealing herself beneath her umbrella, while her husband fanned his face with an immense handkerchief. Behind them came Laurent, who had the sun streaming fiercely on the back of his neck, without appearing to notice it. He whistled and kicked the stones before him as he strolled along. Now and again there was a fierce glint in his eyes as he watched Therese's swinging hips.

On reaching Saint-Ouen, they lost no time in looking for a cluster of trees, a patch of green grass in the shade. Crossing the water to an island, they plunged into a bit of underwood. The fallen leaves covered the ground with a russety bed which cracked beneath their feet with sharp, quivering sounds. Innumerable trunks of trees rose up erect, like clusters of small gothic columns; the branches descended to the foreheads of the three holiday makers, whose only view was the expiring copper-like foliage, and the black and white stems of the aspens and oaks. They were in the wilderness, in a melancholy corner, in a narrow clearing that was silent and fresh. All around them they heard the murmur of the Seine.

Camille having selected a dry spot, seated himself on the ground, after lifting up the skirt of his frock coat; while Therese, amid a loud crumpling of petticoats, had just flung herself among the leaves. Laurent lay on his stomach with his chin resting on the ground.

They remained three hours in this clearing, waiting until it became cooler, to take a run in the country before dinner. Camille talked about his office, and related silly stories; then, feeling fatigued, he let himself fall backward and went to sleep with the rim of his hat over his eyes. Therese had closed her eyelids some time previously, feigning slumber.

Laurent, who felt wide awake, and was tired of his recumbent position, crept up behind her and kissed her shoe and ankle. For a month his life had been chaste and this walk in the sun had set him on fire. Here he was, in a hidden retreat, and unable to hold to his breast the woman who was really his. Her husband might wake up and all his prudent calculations would be ruined by this obstacle of a man. So he lay, flat on the ground, hidden by his lover's skirts, trembling with exasperation as he pressed kiss after kiss upon the shoe and white stocking. Therese made no movement. Laurent thought she was asleep.

He rose to his feet and stood with his back to a tree. Then he perceived that the young woman was gazing into space with her great, sparkling eyes wide open. Her face, lying between her arms, with her hands clasped above her head, was deadly pale, and wore an expression of frigid rigidity. Therese was musing. Her fixed eyes resembled dark, unfathomable depths, where naught was visible save night. She did not move, she did not cast a glance at Laurent, who stood erect behind her.

Her sweetheart contemplated her, and was almost affrighted to see her so motionless and mute. He would have liked to have bent forward, and closed those great open eyes with a kiss. But Camille lay asleep close at hand. This poor creature, with his body twisted out of shape, displaying his lean proportions, was gently snoring. Under the hat, half concealing his face, could be seen his mouth contorted into a silly grimace in his slumber. A few short reddish hairs on a bony chin sullied his livid skin, and his head being thrown backward, his thin wrinkled neck appeared, with Adam's apple standing out prominently in brick red in the centre, and rising at each snore. Camille, spread out on the ground in this fashion, looked contemptible and vile.

Laurent who looked at him, abruptly raised his heel. He was going to crush his face at one blow.

Therese restrained a cry. She went a shade paler than before, closed her eyes and turned her head away as if to avoid being bespattered with blood.

Laurent, for a few seconds, remained with his heel in the air, above the face of the slumbering Camille. Then slowly, straightening his leg, he moved a few paces away. He reflected that this would be a form of murder such as an idiot would choose. This pounded head would have set all the police on him. If he wanted to get rid of Camille, it was solely for the purpose of marrying Therese. It was his intention to bask in the sun, after the crime, like the murderer of the wagoner, in the story related by old Michaud.

He went as far as the edge of the water, and watched the running river in a stupid manner. Then, he abruptly turned into the underwood again. He had just arranged a plan. He had thought of a mode of murder that would be convenient, and without danger to himself.

He awoke the sleeper by tickling his nose with a straw. Camille sneezed, got up, and pronounced the joke a capital one. He liked Laurent on account of his tomfoolery, which made him laugh. He now roused his wife, who kept her eyes closed. When she had risen to her feet, and shaken her skirt, which was all crumpled, and covered with dry leaves, the party quitted the clearing, breaking the small branches they found in their way.

They left the island, and walked along the roads, along the byways crowded with groups in Sunday finery. Between the hedges ran girls in light frocks; a number of boating men passed by singing; files of middle-class couples, of elderly persons, of clerks and shopmen with their wives, walked the short steps, besides the ditches. Each roadway seemed like a populous, noisy street. The sun alone maintained its great tranquility. It was descending towards the horizon, casting on the reddened trees and white thoroughfares immense sheets of pale light. Penetrating freshness began to fall from the quivering sky.

Camille had ceased giving his arm to Therese. He was chatting with Laurent, laughing at the jests, at the feats of strength of his friend, who leapt the ditches and raised huge stones above his head. The young woman, on the other side of the road, advanced with her head bent forward, stooping down from time to time to gather an herb. When she had fallen behind, she stopped and observed her sweetheart and husband in the distance.

"Heh! Aren't you hungry?" shouted Camille at her.

"Yes," she replied.

"Then, come on!" said he.

Therese was not hungry; but felt tired and uneasy. She was in ignorance as to the designs of Laurent, and her lower limbs were trembling with anxiety.

The three, returning to the riverside, found a restaurant, where they seated themselves at table on a sort of terrace formed of planks in an indifferent eating-house reeking with the odour of grease and wine. This place resounded with cries, songs, and the clatter of plates and dishes. In each private room and public saloon, were parties talking in loud voices, and the thin partitions gave vibrating sonority to all this riot. The waiters, ascending to the upper rooms, caused the staircase to shake.

Above, on the terrace, the puffs of air from the river drove away the smell of fat. Therese, leaning over the balustrade, observed the quay. To right and left, extended two lines of wine-shops and shanties of show-men. Beneath the arbours in the gardens of the former, amid the few remaining yellow leaves, one perceived the white tablecloths, the dabs of black formed by men's coats, and the brilliant skirts of women. People passed to and fro, bareheaded, running, and laughing; and with the bawling noise of the crowd, was mingled the lamentable strains of the barrel organs. An odour of dust and frying food hung in the calm air.

Below Therese, some tarts from the Latin Quarter were dancing in a ring on a patch of worn turf singing an infantine roundelay. With hats fallen on their shoulders, and hair unbound, they held one another by the hands, playing like little children. They still managed to find a small thread of fresh voice, and their pale countenances, ruffled by brutal caresses, became tenderly coloured with virgin-like blushes, while their great impure eyes filled with moisture. A few students, smoking clean clay pipes, who were watching them as they turned round, greeted them with ribald jests.

And beyond, on the Seine, on the hillocks, descended the serenity of night, a sort of vague bluish mist, which bathed the trees in transparent vapour.

"Heh! Waiter!" shouted Laurent, leaning over the banister, "what about this dinner?"

Then, changing his mind, he turned to Camille and said:

"I say, Camille, let us go for a pull on the river before sitting down to table. It will give them time to roast the fowl. We shall be bored to death waiting an hour here."

"As you like," answered Camille carelessly. "But Therese is hungry."

"No, no, I can wait," hastened to say the young woman, at whom

Laurent was fixedly looking.

All three went downstairs again. Passing before the rostrum where the lady cashier was seated, they retained a table, and decided on a menu, saying they would return in an hour. As the host let out pleasure boats, they asked him to come and detach one. Laurent selected a skiff, which appeared so light that Camille was terrified by its fragility.

"The deuce," said he, "we shall have to be careful not to move about in this, otherwise we shall get a famous ducking."

The truth was that the clerk had a horrible dread of the water. At Vernon, his sickly condition did not permit him, when a child, to go and dabble in the Seine. Whilst his schoolfellows ran and threw themselves into the river, he lay abed between a couple of warm blankets. Laurent had become an intrepid swimmer, and an indefatigable oarsman. Camille had preserved that terror for deep water which is inherent in women and children. He tapped the end of the boat with his foot to make sure of its solidity.

"Come, get in," cried Laurent with a laugh, "you're always trembling."

Camille stepped over the side, and went staggering to seat himself at the stern. When he felt the planks under him, he was at ease, and joked to show his courage.

Therese had remained on the bank, standing grave and motionless beside her sweetheart, who held the rope. He bent down, and rapidly murmured in an undertone:

"Be careful. I am going to pitch him in the river. Obey me. I answer for everything."

The young woman turned horribly pale. She remained as if riveted to the ground. She was rigid, and her eyes had opened wider.

"Get into the boat," Laurent murmured again.

She did not move. A terrible struggle was passing within her. She strained her will with all her might, to avoid bursting into sobs, and falling to the ground.

"Ah! ah!" cried Camille. "Laurent, just look at Therese. It's she who is afraid. She'll get in; no, she won't get in."

He had now spread himself out on the back seat, his two arms on the sides of the boat, and was showing off with fanfaronade. The chuckles of this poor man were like cuts from a whip to Therese, lashing and urging her on. She abruptly sprang into the boat, remaining in the bows. Laurent grasped the skulls. The skiff left the bank, advancing slowly towards the isles.

Twilight came. Huge shadows fell from the trees, and the water ran black at the edges. In the middle of the river were great, pale, silver trails. The boat was soon in full steam. There, all the sounds of the quays softened; the singing, and the cries came vague and melancholy, with sad languidness. The odour of frying and dust had passed away. The air freshened. It turned cold.

Laurent, resting on his skulls, allowed the boat to drift along in the current.

Opposite, rose the great reddish mass of trees on the islands. The two sombre brown banks, patched with grey, were like a couple of broad bands stretching towards the horizon. The water and sky seemed as if cut from the same whitish piece of material. Nothing looks more painfully calm than an autumn twilight. The sun rays pale in the quivering air, the old trees cast their leaves. The country, scorched by the ardent beams of summer, feels death coming with the first cold winds. And, in the sky, there are plaintive sighs of despair. Night falls from above, bringing winding sheets in its shade.

The party were silent. Seated at the bottom of the boat drifting with the stream, they watched the final gleams of light quitting the tall branches. They approached the islands. The great russety masses grew sombre; all the landscape became simplified in the twilight; the Seine, the sky, the islands, the slopes were naught but brown and grey patches which faded away amidst milky fog.

Camille, who had ended by lying down on his stomach, with his head over the water, dipped his hands in the river.

"The deuce! How cold it is!" he exclaimed. "It would not be pleasant to go in there head foremost."

Laurent did not answer. For an instant he had been observing the two banks of the river with uneasiness. He advanced his huge hands to his knees, tightly compressing his lips. Therese, rigid and motionless, with her head thrown slightly backward, waited.

The skiff was about to enter a small arm of the river, that was sombre and narrow, penetrating between two islands. Behind one of these islands could be distinguished the softened melody of a boating party who seemed to be ascending the Seine. Up the river in the distance, the water was free.

Then Laurent rose and grasped Camille round the body. The clerk burst into laughter.

"Ah, no, you tickle me," said he, "none of those jokes. Look here, stop; you'll make me fall over."

Laurent grasped him tighter, and gave a jerk. Camille turning round, perceived the terrifying face of his friend, violently agitated. He failed to understand. He was seized with vague terror. He wanted to shout, and felt a rough hand seize him by the throat. With the instinct of an animal on the defensive, he rose to his knees, clutching the side of the boat, and struggled for a few seconds.

"Therese! Therese!" he called in a stifling, sibilant voice.

The young woman looked at him, clinging with both hands to the seat. The skiff creaked and danced upon the river. She could not close her eyes, a frightful contraction kept them wide open riveted on the hideous struggle. She remained rigid and mute.

"Therese! Therese!" again cried the unfortunate man who was in the throes of death.

At this final appeal, Therese burst into sobs. Her nerves had given way. The attack she had been dreading, cast her to the bottom of the boat, where she remained doubled up in a swoon, and as if dead.

Laurent continued tugging at Camille, pressing with one hand on his throat. With the other hand he ended by tearing his victim away from the side of the skiff, and held him up in the air, in his powerful arms, like a child. As he bent down his head, his victim, mad with rage and terror, twisted himself round, and reaching forward with his teeth, buried them in the neck of his aggressor. And when the murderer, restraining a yell of pain, abruptly flung the clerk into the river, the latter carried a piece of his flesh away with him.

Camille fall into the water with a shriek. He returned to the surface two or three times, uttering cries that were more and more hollow.

Laurent, without losing a second, raised the collar of his coat to hide his wound. Then seizing the unconscious Therese in his arms, he capsized the skiff with his foot, as he fell into the Seine with the young woman, whom he supported on the surface, whilst calling in a lamentable voice for help.

The boating party he had heard singing behind the point of the island, understanding that an accident had happened, advanced with long, rapid strokes of the oars, and rescued the immerged couple. While

Therese was laid on a bench, Laurent gave vent to his despair at the death of his friend. Plunging into the water again, he searched for Camille in places where he knew he was not to be found, and returned in tears, wringing his hands, and tearing his hair, while the boating party did their best to calm and console him.

"It is all my fault," he exclaimed. "I ought never to have allowed that poor fellow to dance and move about as he did. At a certain moment we all three found ourselves on one side of the boat, and we capsized. As we fell into the water, he shouted out to me to save his wife."

In accordance with what usually happens under similar circumstances, three or four young fellows among the boating party, maintained that they had witnessed the accident.

"We saw you well enough," said they. "And, then, hang it all, a boat is not so firm as a dancing floor. Ah! the poor little woman, it'll be a nice awakening for her."

They took their oars, and towing the capsized skiff behind them, conducted Therese and Laurent to the restaurant, where the dinner was ready to be served.

The restaurant keeper and his wife were worthy people who placed their wardrobe at the service of the drenched pair. When Therese recovered consciousness, she had a nervous attack, and burst into heartrending sobs. It became necessary to put her to bed. Nature assisted the sinister comedy that had just been performed.

As soon as the young woman became calmer, Laurent entrusting her to the care of the host and his wife, set out to return to Paris, where he wished to arrive alone to break the frightful intelligence to Madame Raquin, with all possible precautions. The truth was that he feared the nervous feverish excitement of Therese, and preferred to give her time to reflect, and learn her part.

It was the boating men who sat down to the dinner prepared for Camille.

CHAPTER XII

Laurent, in the dark corner of the omnibus that took him back to Paris, continued perfecting his plan. He was almost certain of impunity, and he felt heavy, anxious joy, the joy of having got over the crime. On reaching the gate at Clichy, he hailed a cab, and drove to the residence of old Michaud in the Rue de Seine. It was nine o'clock at night when he arrived.

He found the former commissary of police at table, in the company of Olivier and Suzanne. The motive of his visit was to seek protection, in case he should be suspected, and also to escape breaking the frightful news to Madame Raquin himself. Such an errand was strangely repugnant to him. He anticipated encountering such terrible despair that he feared he would be unable to play his part with sufficient tears. Then the grief of this mother weighed upon him, although at the bottom of his heart, he cared but little about it.

When Michaud saw him enter, clothed in coarse-looking garments that were too tight for him, he questioned him with his eyes, and Laurent gave an account of the accident in a broken voice, as if exhausted with grief and fatigue.

"I have come to you," said he in conclusion, "because I do not know what to do about the two poor women so cruelly afflicted. I dare not go to the bereaved mother alone, and want you to accompany me."

As he spoke, Olivier looked at him fixedly, and with so straight a glance that he terrified him. The murderer had flung himself head down among these people belonging to the police, with an audacity calculated to save him. But he could not repress a shudder as he felt their eyes examining him. He saw distrust where there was naught but stupor and pity.

Suzanne weaker and paled than usual, seemed ready to faint. Olivier, who was alarmed at the idea of death, but whose heart remained absolutely cold, made a grimace expressing painful surprise, while by habit he scrutinised the countenance of Laurent, without having the least suspicion of the sinister truth. As to old Michaud, he uttered exclamations of fright, commiseration, and astonishment; he fidgeted on his chair, joined his hands together, and cast up his eyes to the ceiling.

"Ah! good heavens," said he in a broken voice, "ah! good heavens, what a frightful thing! To leave one's home, and die, like that, all of a sudden. It's horrible. And that poor Madame Raquin, his mother, whatever shall we say to her? Certainly, you were quite right to come and find us. We will go with you."

Rising from his seat, he walked hither and thither about the apartment, stamping with his feet, in search of his hat and walking-stick; and, as he bustled from corner to corner, he made Laurent repeat the details of the catastrophe, giving utterance to fresh exclamations at the end of each sentence.

At last all four went downstairs. On reaching the entrance to the Arcade of the Pont Neuf, Laurent was stopped by Michaud.

"Do not accompany us any further," said he; "your presence would be a sort of brutal avowal which must be avoided. The wretched mother would suspect a misfortune, and this would force us to confess the truth sooner than we ought to tell it to her. Wait for us here."

This arrangement relieved the murderer, who shuddered at the thought of entering the shop in the arcade. He recovered his calm, and began walking up and down the pavement, going and coming, in perfect peace of mind. At moments, he forgot the events that were passing. He looked at the shops, whistled between his teeth, turned round to ogle the women who brushed past him. He remained thus for a full half-hour in the street, recovering his composure more and more.

He had not eaten since the morning, and feeling hungry he entered a pastrycook's and stuffed himself with cakes.

A heartrending scene was passing at the shop in the arcade. Notwithstanding precautions, notwithstanding the soft, friendly sentences of old Michaud, there came a moment when Madame Raquin understood that her son had met with misfortune. From that moment, she insisted on knowing the truth with such a passionate outburst of despair, with such a violent flow of tears and shrieks, that her old friend could not avoid giving way to her.

And when she learnt the truth, her grief was tragic. She gave hollow sobs, she received shocks that threw her backward, in a distracting attack of terror and anguish. She remained there choking, uttering from time to time a piercing scream amidst the profound roar of her affliction. She would have dragged herself along the ground, had not Suzanne taken her round the waist, weeping on her knees, and raising her pale countenance towards her. Olivier and his father on their feet, unnerved and mute, turned aside their heads, being disagreeably affected at this painful sight which wounded them in their egotism.

The poor mother saw her son rolling along in the thick waters of the Seine, a rigid and horribly swollen corpse; while at the same time, she perceived him a babe, in his cradle, when she drove away death bending over him. She had brought him back into the world on more than ten occasions; she loved him for all the love she had bestowed on him during thirty years. And now he had met his death far away from her, all at once, in the cold and dirty water, like a dog.

Then she remembered the warm blankets in which she had enveloped him. What care she had taken of her boy! What a tepid temperature he had been reared in! How she had coaxed and fondled him! And all this to see him one day miserably drown himself! At these thoughts Madame Raquin felt a tightening at the throat, and she hoped she was going to die, strangled by despair.

Old Michaud hastened to withdraw. Leaving Suzanne behind to look after the mercer, he and Olivier went to find Laurent, so that they might hurry to Saint-Ouen with all speed.

During the journey, they barely exchanged a few words. Each of them buried himself in a corner of the cab which jolted along over the stones. There they remained motionless and mute in the obscurity that prevailed within the vehicle. Ever and anon a rapid flash from a gas lamp, cast a bright gleam on their faces. The sinister event that had brought them together, threw a sort of dismal dejection upon them.

When they at length arrived at the restaurant beside the river, they found Therese in bed with burning head and hands. The landlord told them in an undertone, that the young woman had a violent fever. The truth was that Therese, feeling herself weak in character and wanting in courage, feared she might confess the crime in one of her nervous attacks, and had decided to feign illness.

Maintaining sullen silence, she kept her lips and eyes closed, unwilling to see anyone lest she should speak. With the bedclothes to her chin, her face half concealed by the pillow, she made herself quite small, anxiously listening to all that was said around her. And, amidst the reddish gleam that passed beneath her closed lids, she could still see Camille and Laurent struggling at the side of the boat. She perceived her husband, livid, horrible, increased in height, rearing up straight above the turbid water, and this implacable vision heightened the feverish heat of her blood.

72

Old Michaud endeavoured to speak to her and console her. But she made a movement of impatience, and turning round, broke out into a fresh fit of sobbing.

"Leave her alone, sir," said the restaurant keeper, "she shudders at the slightest sound. You see, she wants rest."

Below, in the general room, was a policeman drawing up a statement of the accident. Michaud and his son went downstairs, followed by Laurent. When Olivier had made himself known as an upper official at the Prefecture of Police, everything was over in ten minutes. The boating men, who were still there, gave an account of the drowning in its smallest details, describing how the three holiday-makers had fallen into the water, as if they themselves had witnessed the misfortune. Had Olivier and his father the least suspicion, it would have been dispelled at once by this testimony.

But they had not doubted the veracity of Laurent for an instant. On the contrary, they introduced him to the policeman as the best friend of the victim, and they were careful to see inserted in the report, that the young man had plunged into the water to save Camille Raquin. The following day, the newspapers related the accident with a great display of detail: the unfortunate mother, the inconsolable widow, the noble and courageous friend, nothing was missing from this event of the day, which went the round of the Parisian press, and then found an echo in the provinces.

When the report was completed, Laurent experienced lively joy, which penetrated his being like new life. From the moment his victim had buried his teeth in his neck, he had been as if stiffened, acting mechanically, according to a plan arranged long in advance. The instinct of self-preservation alone impelled him, dictating to him his words, affording him advice as to his gestures.

At this hour, in the face of the certainty of impunity, the blood resumed flowing in his veins with delicious gentleness. The police had passed beside his crime, and had seen nothing. They had been duped, for they had just acquitted him. He was saved. This thought caused him to experience a feeling of delightful moisture all along his body, a warmth that restored flexibility to his limbs and to his intelligence. He continued to act his part of a weeping friend with incomparable science and assurance. At the bottom of his heart, he felt brutal satisfaction; and he thought of Therese who was in bed in the room above.

"We cannot leave this unhappy woman here," said he to Michaud. "She is perhaps threatened with grave illness. We must positively take her back to Paris. Come, let us persuade her to accompany us."

Upstairs, he begged and prayed of Therese to rise and dress, and allow herself to be conducted to the Arcade of the Pont Neuf. When the young woman heard the sound of his voice, she started, and stared at him with eyes wide open. She seemed as if crazy, and was shuddering. Painfully she raised herself into a sitting posture without answering. The men quitted the room, leaving her alone with the wife of the restaurant keeper. When ready to start, she came downstairs staggering, and was assisted into the cab by Olivier.

The journey was a silent one. Laurent, with perfect audacity and impudence, slipped his hand along the skirt of Therese and caught her fingers. He was seated opposite her, in a floating shadow, and could not see her face which she kept bowed down on her breast. As soon as he had grasped her hand, he pressed it vigorously, retaining it until they reached the Rue Mazarine. He felt the hand tremble; but it was not withdrawn. On the contrary it ever and anon gave a sudden caress.

These two hands, one in the other, were burning; the moist palms adhered, and the fingers tightly held together, were hurt at each pressure. It seemed to Laurent and Therese that the blood from one penetrated the chest of the other, passing through their joined fists. These fists became a live fire whereon their lives were boiling. Amidst the night, amidst the heartrending silence that prevailed, the furious grips they exchanged, were like a crushing weight cast on the head of Camille to keep him under water.

When the cab stopped, Michaud and his son got out the first, and Laurent bending towards his sweetheart gently murmured:

"Be strong, Therese. We have a long time to wait. Recollect."

Then the young woman opened her lips for the first time since the death of her husband.

"Oh! I shall recollect," said she with a shudder, and in a voice light as a puff of breath.

Olivier extended his hand, inviting her to get down. On this occasion, Laurent went as far as the shop. Madame Raquin was abed, a prey to violent delirium. Therese dragged herself to her room, where Suzanne had barely time to undress her before she gave way. Tranquillised, perceiving that everything was proceeding as well as he could

wish, Laurent withdrew, and slowly gained his wretched den in the rue
Saint-Victor.

It was past midnight. Fresh air circulated in the deserted, silent
streets. The young man could hear naught but his own footsteps resounding on the pavement. The nocturnal coolness of the atmosphere
cheered him up; the silence, the darkness gave him sharp sensations of
delight, and he loitered on his way.

At last he was rid of his crime. He had killed Camille. It was a matter that was settled, and would be spoken of no more. He was now
going to lead a tranquil existence, until he could take possession of
Therese. The thought of the murder had at times half choked him, but
now that it was accomplished, he felt a weight removed from his chest,
and breathed at ease, cured of the suffering that hesitation and fear had
given him.

At the bottom of his heart, he was a trifle hebetated. Fatigue had
rendered his limbs and thoughts heavy. He went in to bed and slept
soundly. During his slumber slight nervous crispations coursed over his
face.

CHAPTER XIII

The following morning, Laurent awoke fresh and fit. He had slept well. The cold air entering by the open window, whipped his sluggish blood. He had no clear recollection of the scenes of the previous day, and had it not been for the burning sensation at his neck, he might have thought that he had retired to rest after a calm evening.

But the bite Camille had given him stung as if his skin had been branded with a red-hot iron. When his thoughts settled on the pain this gash caused him, he suffered cruelly. It seemed as though a dozen needles were penetrating little by little into his flesh.

He turned down the collar of his shirt, and examined the wound in a wretched fifteen sous looking-glass hanging against the wall. It formed a red hole, as big as a penny piece. The skin had been torn away, displaying the rosy flesh, studded with dark specks. Streaks of blood had run as far as the shoulder in thin threads that had dried up. The bite looked a deep, dull brown colour against the white skin, and was situated under the right ear. Laurent scrutinised it with curved back and craned neck, and the greenish mirror gave his face an atrocious grimace.

Satisfied with his examination, he had a thorough good wash, saying to himself that the wound would be healed in a few days. Then he dressed, and quietly repaired to his office, where he related the accident in an affected tone of voice. When his colleagues had read the account in the newspapers, he became quite a hero. During a whole week the clerks at the Orleans Railway had no other subject of conversation: they were all proud that one of their staff should have been drowned. Grivet never ceased his remarks on the imprudence of adventuring into the middle of the Seine, when it was so easy to watch the running water from the bridges.

Laurent retained a feeling of intense uneasiness. The decease of Camille had not been formally proved. The husband of Therese was indeed dead, but the murderer would have liked to have found his body, so as to obtain a certificate of death. The day following the accident, a fruitless search had been made for the corpse of the drowned man. It was thought that it had probably gone to the bottom of some hole near the banks of the islands, and men were actively dragging the Seine to get the reward.

In the meantime Laurent imposed on himself the task of passing each morning by the Morgue, on the way to his office. He had made up his mind to attend to the business himself. Notwithstanding that his heart rose with repugnance, notwithstanding the shudders that sometimes ran through his frame, for over a week he went and examined the countenance of all the drowned persons extended on the slabs.

When he entered the place an unsavoury odour, an odour of freshly washed flesh, disgusted him and a chill ran over his skin: the dampness of the walls seemed to add weight to his clothing, which hung more heavily on his shoulders. He went straight to the glass separating the spectators from the corpses, and with his pale face against it, looked. Facing him appeared rows of grey slabs, and upon them, here and there, the naked bodies formed green and yellow, white and red patches. While some retained their natural condition in the rigidity of death, others seemed like lumps of bleeding and decaying meat. At the back, against the wall, hung some lamentable rags, petticoats and trousers, puckered against the bare plaster. Laurent at first only caught sight of the wan ensemble of stones and walls, spotted with dabs of russet and black formed by the clothes and corpses. A melodious sound of running water broke the silence.

Little by little he distinguished the bodies, and went from one to the other. It was only the drowned that interested him. When several human forms were there, swollen and blued by the water, he looked at them eagerly, seeking to recognise Camille. Frequently, the flesh on the faces had gone away by strips, the bones had burst through the mellow skins, the visages were like lumps of boned, boiled beef. Laurent hesitated; he looked at the corpses, endeavouring to discover the lean body of his victim. But all the drowned were stout. He saw enormous stomachs, puffy thighs, and strong round arms. He did not know what to do. He stood there shuddering before those greenish-looking rags, which seemed like mocking him, with their horrible wrinkles.

One morning, he was seized with real terror. For some moments, he had been looking at a corpse, taken from the water, that was small in build and atrociously disfigured. The flesh of this drowned person was so soft and broken-up that the running water washing it, carried it away bit by bit. The jet falling on the face, bored a hole to the left of the nose. And, abruptly, the nose became flat, the lips were detached, showing the white teeth. The head of the drowned man burst out laughing.

Each time Laurent fancied he recognised Camille, he felt a burning sensation in the heart. He ardently desired to find the body of his victim, and he was seized with cowardice when he imagined it before him. His visits to the Morgue filled him with nightmare, with shudders that set him panting for breath. But he shook off his fear, taxing himself with being childish, when he wished to be strong. Still, in spite of himself, his frame revolted, disgust and terror gained possession of his being, as soon as ever he found himself in the dampness, and unsavoury odour of the hall.

When there were no drowned persons on the back row of slabs, he breathed at ease; his repugnance was not so great. He then became a simple spectator, who took strange pleasure in looking death by violence in the face, in its lugubriously fantastic and grotesque attitudes. This sight amused him, particularly when there were women there displaying their bare bosoms. These nudities, brutally exposed, bloodstained, and in places bored with holes, attracted and detained him.

Once he saw a young woman of twenty there, a child of the people, broad and strong, who seemed asleep on the stone. Her fresh, plump, white form displayed the most delicate softness of tint. She was half smiling, with her head slightly inclined on one side. Around her neck she had a black band, which gave her a sort of necklet of shadow. She was a girl who had hanged herself in a fit of love madness.

Each morning, while Laurent was there, he heard behind him the coming and going of the public who entered and left.

The morgue is a sight within reach of everybody, and one to which passers-by, rich and poor alike, treat themselves. The door stands open, and all are free to enter. There are admirers of the scene who go out of their way so as not to miss one of these performances of death. If the slabs have nothing on them, visitors leave the building disappointed, feeling as if they had been cheated, and murmuring between their teeth; but when they are fairly well occupied, people crowd in front of them and treat themselves to cheap emotions; they express horror, they joke, they applaud or whistle, as at the theatre, and withdraw satisfied, declaring the Morgue a success on that particular day.

Laurent soon got to know the public frequenting the place, that mixed and dissimilar public who pity and sneer in common. Workmen looked in on their way to their work, with a loaf of bread and tools under their arms. They considered death droll. Among them were comical companions of the workshops who elicited a smile from the on-lookers by making witty remarks about the faces of each corpse. They styled those who had been burnt to death, coalmen; the hanged, the murdered, the drowned, the bodies that had been stabbed or crushed, excited their jeering vivacity, and their voices, which slightly trembled, stammered out comical sentences amid the shuddering silence of the hall.

There came persons of small independent means, old men who were thin and shrivelled-up, idlers who entered because they had noth-ing to do, and who looked at the bodies in a silly manner with the pouts of peaceful, delicate-minded men. Women were there in great num-bers: young work-girls, all rosy, with white linen, and clean petticoats, who tripped along briskly from one end of the glazed partition to the other, opening great attentive eyes, as if they were before the dressed shop window of a linendraper. There were also women of the lower or-ders looking stupefied, and giving themselves lamentable airs; and well-dressed ladies, carelessly dragging their silk gowns along the floor.

On a certain occasion Laurent noticed one of the latter standing at a few paces from the glass, and pressing her cambric handkerchief to her nostrils. She wore a delicious grey silk skirt with a large black lace mantle; her face was covered by a veil, and her gloved hands seemed quite small and delicate. Around her hung a gentle perfume of violet.

She stood scrutinising a corpse. On a slab a few paces away, was stretched the body of a great, big fellow, a mason who had recently killed himself on the spot by falling from a scaffolding. He had a broad chest, large short muscles, and a white, well-nourished body; death had made a marble statue of him. The lady examined him, turned him round and weighed him, so to say, with her eyes. For a time, she seemed quite absorbed in the contemplation of this man. She raised a corner of her veil for one last look. Then she withdrew.

At moments, bands of lads arrived—young people between twelve and fifteen, who leant with their hands against the glass, nudging one another with their elbows, and making brutal observations.

At the end of a week, Laurent became disheartened. At night he dreamt of the corpses he had seen in the morning. This suffering, this daily disgust which he imposed on himself, ended by troubling him to such a point, that he resolved to pay only two more visits to the place. The next day, on entering the Morgue, he received a violent shock in the chest. Opposite him, on a slab, Camille lay looking at him, extended on his back, his head raised, his eyes half open.

The murderer slowly approached the glass, as if attracted there, unable to detach his eyes from his victim. He did not suffer; he merely experienced a great inner chill, accompanied by slight pricks on his skin. He would have thought that he would have trembled more violently. For fully five minutes, he stood motionless, lost in unconscious contemplation, engraving, in spite of himself, in his memory, all the horrible lines, all the dirty colours of the picture he had before his eyes.

Camille was hideous. He had been a fortnight in the water. His face still appeared firm and rigid; the features were preserved, but the skin had taken a yellowish, muddy tint. The thin, bony, and slightly tumefied head, wore a grimace. It was a trifle inclined on one side, with the hair sticking to the temples, and the lids raised, displaying the dull globes of the eyes. The twisted lips were drawn to a corner of the mouth in an atrocious grin; and a piece of blackish tongue appeared between the white teeth. This head, which looked tanned and drawn out lengthwise, while preserving a human appearance, had remained all the more frightful with pain and terror.

The body seemed a mass of ruptured flesh; it had suffered horribly. You could feel that the arms no longer held to their sockets; and the clavicles were piercing the skin of the shoulders. The ribs formed black bands on the greenish chest; the left side, ripped open, was gaping amidst dark red shreds. All the torso was in a state of putrefaction. The extended legs, although firmer, were daubed with dirty patches. The feet dangled down.

Laurent gazed at Camille. He had never yet seen the body of a drowned person presenting such a dreadful aspect. The corpse, moreover, looked pinched. It had a thin, poor appearance. It had shrunk up in its decay, and the heap it formed was quite small. Anyone might have guessed that it belonged to a clerk at 1,200 francs a year, who was stupid and sickly, and who had been brought up by his mother on infusions. This miserable frame, which had grown to maturity between warm blankets, was now shivering on a cold slab.

When Laurent could at last tear himself from the poignant curiosity that kept him motionless and gaping before his victim, he went out and begun walking rapidly along the quay. And as he stepped out, he repeated:

"That is what I have done. He is hideous."

A smell seemed to be following him, the smell that the putrefying body must be giving off.

He went to find old Michaud, and told him he had just recognized Camille lying on one of the slabs in the Morgue. The formalities were performed, the drowned man was buried, and a certificate of death delivered. Laurent, henceforth at ease, felt delighted to be able to bury his crime in oblivion, along with the vexatious and painful scenes that had followed it.

CHAPTER XIV

The shop in the Arcade of the Pont Neuf remained closed for three days. When it opened again, it appeared darker and damper. The shop-front display, which the dust had turned yellow, seemed to be wearing the mourning of the house; the various articles were scattered at sixes and sevens in the dirty windows. Behind the linen caps hanging from the rusty iron rods, the face of Therese presented a more olive, a more sallow pallidness, and the immobility of sinister calm.

All the gossips in the arcade were moved to pity. The dealer in imitation jewelry pointed out the emaciated profile of the young widow to each of her customers, as an interesting and lamentable curiosity.

For three days, Madame Raquin and Therese had remained in bed without speaking, and without even seeing one another. The old mercer, propped up by pillows in a sitting posture, gazed vaguely before her with the eyes of an idiot. The death of her son had been like a blow on the head that had felled her senseless to the ground. For hours she remained tranquil and inert, absorbed in her despair; then she was at times seized with attacks of weeping, shrieking and delirium.

Therese in the adjoining room, seemed to sleep. She had turned her face to the wall, and drawn the sheet over her eyes. There she lay stretched out at full length, rigid and mute, without a sob raising the bed-clothes. It looked as if she was concealing the thoughts that made her rigid in the darkness of the alcove.

Suzanne, who attended to the two women, went feebly from one to the other, gently dragging her feet along the floor, bending her wax-like countenance over the two couches, without succeeding in persuading Therese, who had sudden fits of impatience, to turn round, or in consoling Madame Raquin, whose tears began to flow as soon as a voice drew her from her prostration.

On the third day, Therese, rapidly and with a sort of feverish decision, threw the sheet from her, and seated herself up in bed. She thrust back her hair from her temples, and for a moment remained with her hands to her forehead and her eyes fixed, seeming still to reflect. Then, she sprang to the carpet. Her limbs were shivering, and red with fever; large livid patches marbled her skin, which had become wrinkled in places as if she had lost flesh. She had grown older.

Suzanne, on entering the room, was struck with surprise to find her up. In a placid, drawling tone, she advised her to go to bed again, and continue resting. Therese paid no heed to her, but sought her clothes and put them on with hurried, trembling gestures. When she was dressed, she went and looked at herself in a glass, rubbing her eyes, and passing her hands over her countenance, as if to efface something. Then, without pronouncing a syllable, she quickly crossed the dining-room and entered the apartment occupied by Madame Raquin.

She caught the old mercer in a moment of doltish calm. When Therese appeared, she turned her head following the movements of the young widow with her eyes, while the latter came and stood before her, mute and oppressed. The two women contemplated one another for some seconds, the niece with increasing anxiety, the aunt with painful efforts of memory. Madame Raquin, at last remembering, stretched out her trembling arms, and, taking Therese by the neck, ex-claimed:

"My poor child, my poor Camille!"

She wept, and her tears dried on the burning skin of the young widow, who concealed her own dry eyes in the folds of the sheet. Therese remained bending down, allowing the old mother to exhaust her outburst of grief. She had dreaded this first interview ever since the murder; and had kept in bed to delay it, to reflect at ease on the ter-rible part she had to play.

When she perceived Madame Raquin more calm, she busied herself about her, advising her to rise, and go down to the shop. The old mer-cer had almost fallen into dotage. The abrupt apparition of her niece had brought about a favourable crisis that had just restored her mem-ory, and the consciousness of things and beings around her. She thanked Suzanne for her attention. Although weakened, she talked, and had ceased wandering, but she spoke in a voice so full of sadness that at moments she was half choked. She watched the movements of Therese with sudden fits of tears; and would then call her to the bed-side, and embrace her amid more sobs, telling her in a suffocating tone that she, now, had nobody but her in the world.

In the evening, she consented to get up, and make an effort to eat. Therese then saw what a terrible shock her aunt had received. The legs of the old lady had become so ponderous that she required a stick to assist her to drag herself into the dining-room, and there she thought the walls were vacillating around her.

Nevertheless, the following day she wished the shop to be opened. She feared she would go mad if she continued to remain alone in her room. She went down the wooden staircase with heavy tread, placing her two feet on each step, and seated herself behind the counter. From that day forth, she remained riveted there in placid affliction.

Therese, beside her, mused and waited. The shop resumed its gloomy calm.

CHAPTER XV

Laurent resumed calling of an evening, every two or three days, remaining in the shop talking to Madame Raquin for half an hour. Then he went off without looking Therese in the face. The old mercer regarded him as the rescuer of her niece, as a noble-hearted young man who had done his utmost to restore her son to her, and she welcomed him with tender kindness.

One Thursday evening, when Laurent happened to be there, old Michaud and Grivet entered. Eight o'clock was striking. The clerk and the former commissary of police had both thought, independently of one another, that they could resume their dear custom, without appearing importunate, and they arrived at the same moment, as if urged by the same impulse. Behind them, came Olivier and Suzanne.

Everyone went upstairs to the dining-room. Madame Raquin who expected nobody, hastened to light the lamp, and prepare the tea. When all were seated round the table, each before a cup, when the box of dominoes had been emptied on the board, the old mother, with the past suddenly brought back to her, looked at her guests, and burst into sobs. There was a vacant place, that of her son.

This despair cast a chill upon the company and annoyed them. Every countenance wore an air of egotistic beatitude. These people fell ill at ease, having no longer the slightest recollection of Camille alive in their hearts.

"Come, my dear lady," exclaimed old Michaud, slightly impatiently, "you must not give way to despair like that. You will make yourself ill."

"We are all mortal," affirmed Grivet.

"Your tears will not restore your son to you," sententiously observed Olivier.

"Do not cause us pain, I beg you," murmured Suzanne.

And as Madame Raquin sobbed louder, unable to restrain her tears, Michaud resumed:

"Come, come, have a little courage. You know we come here to give you some distraction. Then do not let us feel sad. Let us try to forget. We are playing two sous a game. Eh! What do you say?"

The mercer stifled her sobs with a violent effort. Perhaps she was conscious of the happy egotism of her guests. She dried her tears, but was still quite upset. The dominoes trembled in her poor hands, and the moisture in her eyes prevented her seeing.

The game began.

Laurent and Therese had witnessed this brief scene in a grave and impassive manner. The young man was delighted to see these Thursday evenings resumed. He ardently desired them to be continued, aware that he would have need of these gatherings to attain his end. Besides, without asking himself the reason, he felt more at ease among these few persons whom he knew, and it gave him courage to look Therese in the face.

The young woman, attired in black, pale and meditative, seemed to him to possess a beauty that he had hitherto ignored. He was happy to meet her eyes, and to see them rest upon his own with courageous fixedness. Therese still belonged to him, heart and soul.

CHAPTER XVI

A fortnight passed. The bitterness of the first hours was softening; each day brought additional tranquillity and calm; life resumed its course with weary languidness, and with the monotonous intellectual insensibility which follows great shocks. At the commencement, Laurent and Therese allowed themselves to drift into this new existence which was transforming them; within their beings was proceeding a silent labour which would require analysing with extreme delicacy if one desired to mark all its phases.

It was not long before Laurent came every night to the shop as formerly. But he no longer dined there, he no longer made the place a lounge during the entire evening. He arrived at half-past nine, and remained until he had put up the shutters. It seemed as if he was accomplishing a duty in placing himself at the service of the two women. If he happened occasionally to neglect the tiresome job, he apologised with the humility of a valet the following day. On Thursdays he assisted Madame Raquin to light the fire, to do the honours of the house, and displayed all kinds of gentle attentions that charmed the old mercer.

Therese peacefully watched the activity of his movements round about her. The pallidness of her face had departed. She appeared in better health, more smiling and gentle. It was only rarely that her lips, becoming pinched in a nervous contraction, produced two deep pleats which conveyed to her countenance a strange expression of grief and fright.

The two sweethearts no longer sought to see one another in private. Not once did they suggest a meeting, nor did they ever furtively exchange a kiss. The murder seemed to have momentarily appeased their warmth. In killing Camille, they had succeeded in satisfying their passion. Their crime appeared to have given them a keen pleasure that sickened and disgusted them of their embraces.

They had a thousand facilities for enjoying the freedom that had been their dream, and the attainment of which had urged them on to murder. Madame Raquin, impotent and childish, ceased to be an obstacle. The house belonged to them. They could go abroad where they pleased. But love did not trouble them, its fire had died out. They remained there, calmly talking, looking at one another without reddening and without a thrill. They even avoided being alone. In their intimacy, they found nothing to say, and both were afraid that they appeared too cold. When they exchanged a pressure of the hand, they experienced a sort of discomfort at the touch of their skins.

Both imagined they could explain what made them so indifferent and alarmed when face to face with one another. They put the coldness of their attitude down to prudence. Their calm, according to them, was the result of great caution on their part. They pretended they desired this tranquillity, and somnolence of their hearts. On the other hand, they regarded the repugnance, the uncomfortable feeling experienced as a remains of terror, as the secret dread of punishment. Sometimes, forcing themselves to hope, they sought to resume the burning dreams of other days, and were quite astonished to find they had no imagination.

Then, they clung to the idea of their forthcoming marriage. They fancied that having attained their end, without a single fear to trouble them, delivered over to one another, their passion would burn again, and they would taste the delights that had been their dream. This prospect brought them calm, and prevented them descending to the void hollowed out beneath them. They persuaded themselves they loved one another as in the past, and they awaited the moment when they were to be perfectly happy bound together for ever.

Never had Therese possessed so placid a mind. She was certainly becoming better. All her implacable, natural will was giving way. She felt happy at night, alone in her bed; no longer did she find the thin face, and piteous form of Camille at her side to exasperate her. She imagined herself a little girl, a maid beneath the white curtains, lying peacefully amidst the silence and darkness. Her spacious, and slightly cold room rather pleased her, with its lofty ceiling, its obscure corners, and its smack of the cloister.

She even ended by liking the great black wall which rose up before her window. Every night during one entire summer, she remained for hours gazing at the grey stones in this wall, and at the narrow strips of starry sky cut out by the chimneys and roofs. She only thought of Laurent when awakened with a start by nightmare. Then, sitting up, trembling, with dilated eyes, and pressing her nightdress to her, she said to herself that she would not experience these sudden fears, if she had a man lying beside her. She thought of her sweetheart as of a dog who would have guarded and protected her.

Of a daytime, in the shop, she took an interest in what was going on outside; she went out at her own instigation, and no longer lived in sullen revolt, occupied with thoughts of hatred and vengeance. It worried her to sit musing. She felt the necessity of acting and seeing. From morning to night, she watched the people passing through the arcade. The noise, and going and coming diverted her. She became inquisitive and talkative, in a word a woman, for hitherto she had only displayed the actions and ideas of a man.

From her point of observation, she remarked a young man, a student, who lived at an hotel in the neighbourhood, and who passed several times daily before the shop. This youth had a handsome, pale face, with the long hair of a poet, and the moustache of an officer. Therese thought him superior looking. She was in love with him for a week, in love like a schoolgirl. She read novels, she compared the young man to Laurent, and found the latter very coarse and heavy. Her reading revealed to her romantic scenes that, hitherto, she had ignored. She had only loved with blood and nerves, as yet, and she now began to love with her head. Then, one day, the student disappeared. No doubt he had moved. In a few hours Therese had forgotten him.

She now subscribed to a circulating library, and conceived a passion for the heroes of all the stories that passed under her eyes. This sudden love for reading had great influence on her temperament. She acquired nervous sensibility which caused her to laugh and cry without any motive. The equilibrium which had shown a tendency to be established in her, was upset. She fell into a sort of vague meditation. At moments, she became disturbed by thoughts of Camille, and she dreamt of Laurent and fresh love, full of terror and distrust. She again became a prey to anguish. At one moment she sought for the means of marrying her sweetheart at that very instant, at another she had an idea of running away never to see him again.

The novels, which spoke to her of chastity and honour, placed a sort of obstacle between her instincts and her will. She remained the ungovernable creature who had wanted to struggle with the Seine and who had thrown herself violently into illicit love; but she was conscious of goodness and gentleness, she understood the putty face and lifeless attitude of the wife of Olivier, and she knew it was possible to be happy without killing one's husband. Then, she did not see herself in a very good light, and lived in cruel indecision.

Laurent, on his side, passed through several different phases of love and fever. First of all he enjoyed profound tranquility; he seemed as if relieved of an enormous weight. At times he questioned himself with astonishment, fancying he had had a bad dream. He asked himself whether it was really true that he had flung Camille into the water, and had seen his corpse on the slab at the Morgue.

The recollection of his crime caused him strange surprise; never could he have imagined himself capable of murder. He so prudent, so cowardly, shuddered at the mere thought, ice-like beads of perspiration stood out on his forehead when he reflected that the authorities might have discovered his crime and guillotined him. Then he felt the cold knife on his neck. So long as he had acted, he had gone straight before him, with the obstinacy and blindness of a brute. Now, he turned round, and at the sight of the gulf he had just cleared, grew faint with terror.

"Assuredly, I must have been drunk," thought he; "that woman must have intoxicated me with caresses. Good heavens! I was a fool and mad! I risked the guillotine in a business like that. Fortunately it passed off all right. But if it had to be done again, I would not do it."

Laurent lost all his vigor. He became inactive, and more cowardly and prudent than ever. He grew fat and flabby. No one who had studied this great body, piled up in a lump, apparently without bones or muscles, would ever have had the idea of accusing the man of violence and cruelty.

He resumed his former habits. For several months, he proved himself a model clerk, doing his work with exemplary brutishness. At night, he took his meal at a cheap restaurant in the Rue Saint-Victor, cutting his bread into thin slices, masticating his food slowly, making his repast last as long as possible. When it was over, he threw himself back against the wall and smoked his pipe. Anyone might have taken him for a stout, good-natured father. In the daytime, he thought of nothing; at night, he reposed in heavy sleep free from dreams. With his face fat and rosy, his belly full, his brain empty, he felt happy.

His frame seemed dead, and Therese barely entered his mind. Occasionally he thought of her as one thinks of a woman one has to marry later on, in the indefinite future. He patiently awaited the time for his marriage, forgetful of the bride, and dreaming of the new position he would then enjoy. He would leave his office, he would paint for amusement, and saunter about hither and thither. These hopes brought him

night after night, to the shop in the arcade, in spite of the vague discomfort he experienced on entering the place.

One Sunday, with nothing to do and being bored, he went to see his
old school friend, the young painter he had lived with for a time. The
artist was working on a picture of a nude Bacchante sprawled on some
drapery. The model, lying with her head thrown back and her torso
twisted sometimes laughed and threw her bosom forward, stretching
her arms. As Laurent smoked his pipe and chatted with his friend, he
kept his eyes on the model. He took the woman home with him that
evening and kept her as his mistress for many months. The poor girl fell
in love with him. Every morning she went off and posed as a model all
day. Then she came back each evening. She didn't cost Laurent a penny,
keeping herself out of her own earnings. Laurent never bothered to
find out about her, where she went, what she did. She was a steadying
influence in his life, a useful and necessary thing. He never wondered
if he loved her and he never considered that he was being unfaithful to
Therese. He simply felt better and happier.

In the meanwhile the period of mourning that Therese had imposed
on herself, had come to an end, and the young woman put on light-
coloured gowns. One evening, Laurent found her looking younger and
handsomer. But he still felt uncomfortable in her presence. For some
time past, she seemed to him feverish, and full of strange capricious-
ness, laughing and turning sad without reason. This unsettled demeanour alarmed him, for he guessed, in part, what her struggles and
troubles must be like.

He began to hesitate, having an atrocious dread of risking his tranquillity. He was now living peacefully, in wise contentment, and he
feared to endanger the equilibrium of his life, by binding himself to a
nervous woman, whose passion had already driven him crazy. But he
did not reason these matters out, he felt by instinct all the anguish he
would be subjected to, if he made Therese his wife.

The first shock he received, and one that roused him in his slug-
gishness, was the thought that he must at length begin to think of his
marriage. It was almost fifteen months since the death of Camille. For
an instant, Laurent had the idea of not marrying at all, of jilting
Therese. Then he said to himself that it was no good killing a man for
nothing. In recalling the crime, and the terrible efforts he had made to
be the sole possessor of this woman who was now troubling him, he

felt that the murder would become useless and atrocious should he not marry her. Besides, was he not bound to Therese by a bond of blood and horror? Moreover, he feared his accomplice; perhaps, if he failed to marry her, she would go and relate everything to the judicial authorities out of vengeance and jealousy. With these ideas beating in his head the fever settled on him again.

Now, one Sunday the model did not return; no doubt she had found a warmer and more comfortable place to lodge. Laurent was only moderately upset, but he felt a sudden gap in his life without a woman lying beside him at night. In a week his passions rebelled and he began spending entire evenings at the shop again. He watched Therese who was still palpitating from the novels which she read.

After a year of indifferent waiting they both were again tormented by desire. One evening while shutting up the shop, Laurent spoke to Therese in the passage.

"Do you want me to come to your room to-night," he asked passionately.

She started with fear. "No, let's wait. Let's be prudent."

"It seems to me that I've already waited a long time," he went on. "I'm sick of waiting."

Therese, her hands and face burning hot, looked at him wildly. She seemed to hesitate, and then said quickly:

"Let's get married."

CHAPTER XVII

Laurent left the arcade with a strained mind. Therese had filled him with the old longing lusts again. He walked along with his hat in his hand, so as to get the fresh air full in his face.

On reaching the door of his hotel in the Rue Saint-Victor, he was afraid to go upstairs, and remain alone. A childish, inexplicable, unforeseen terror made him fear he would find a man hidden in his garret. Never had he experienced such poltroonery. He did not even seek to account for the strange shudder that ran through him. He entered a wine-shop and remained an hour there, until midnight, motionless and silent at a table, mechanically absorbing great glasses of wine. Thinking of Therese, his anger raged at her refusal to have him in her room that very night. He felt that with her he would not have been afraid.

When the time came for closing the shop, he was obliged to leave. But he went back again to ask for matches. The office of the hotel was on the first floor. Laurent had a long alley to follow and a few steps to ascend, before he could take his candle. This alley, this bit of staircase which was frightfully dark, terrified him. Habitually, he passed boldly through the darkness. But on this particular night he had not even the courage to ring. He said to himself that in a certain recess, formed by the entrance to the cellar, assassins were perhaps concealed, who would suddenly spring at his throat as he passed along.

At last he pulled the bell, and lighting a match, made up his mind to enter the alley. The match went out. He stood motionless, breathless, without the courage to run away, rubbing lucifers against the damp wall in such anxiety that his hand trembled. He fancied he heard voices, and the sound of footsteps before him. The matches broke between his fingers; but he succeeded in striking one. The sulphur began to boil, to set fire to the wood, with a tardiness that increased his distress. In the pale bluish light of the sulphur, in the vacillating glimmer, he fancied he could distinguish monstrous forms. Then the match crackled, and the light became white and clear.

Laurent, relieved, advanced with caution, careful not to be without a match. When he had passed the entrance to the cellar, he clung to the opposite wall where a mass of darkness terrified him. He next briskly scaled the few steps separating him from the office of the hotel, and thought himself safe when he held his candlestick. He ascended to the other floors more gently, holding aloft his candle, lighting all the corners before which he had to pass. The great fantastic shadows that come and go, in ascending a staircase with a light, caused him vague discomfort, as they suddenly rose and disappeared before him.

As soon as he was upstairs, and had rapidly opened his door and shut himself in, his first care was to look under his bed, and make a minute inspection of the room to see that nobody was concealed there. He closed the window in the roof thinking someone might perhaps get in that way, and feeling more calm after taking these measures, he undressed, astonished at his cowardice. He ended by laughing and calling himself a child. Never had he been afraid, and he could not understand this sudden fit of terror.

He went to bed. When he was in the warmth beneath the bedclothes, he again thought of Therese, whom fright had driven from his mind. Do what he would, obstinately close his eyes, endeavour to sleep, he felt his thoughts at work commanding his attention, connecting one with the other, to ever point out to him the advantage he would reap by marrying as soon as possible. Ever and anon he would turn round, saying to himself:

"I must not think any more; I shall have to get up at eight o'clock to-morrow morning to go to my office."

And he made an effort to slip off to sleep. But the ideas returned one by one. The dull labour of his reasoning began again; and he soon found himself in a sort of acute reverie that displayed to him in the depths of his brain, the necessity for his marriage, along with the arguments his desire and prudence advanced in turn, for and against the possession of Therese.

Then, seeing he was unable to sleep, that insomnia kept his body in a state of irritation, he turned on his back, and with his eyes wide open, gave up his mind to the young woman. His equilibrium was upset, he again trembled with violent fever, as formerly. He had an idea of getting up, and returning to the Arcade of the Pont Neuf. He would have the iron gate opened, and Therese would receive him. The thought sent his blood racing.

The lucidity of his reverie was astonishing. He saw himself in the streets walking rapidly beside the houses, and he said to himself:

"I will take this Boulevard, I will cross this Square, so as to arrive there quicker."

Then the iron gate of the arcade grated, he followed the narrow, dark, deserted corridor, congratulating himself at being able to go up to Therese without being seen by the dealer in imitation jewelry. Next he imagined he was in the alley, in the little staircase he had so frequently ascended. He inhaled the sickly odour of the passage, he touched the sticky walls, he saw the dirty shadow that hung about there. And he ascended each step, breathless, and with his ear on the alert. At last he scratched against the door, the door opened, and Therese stood there awaiting him.

His thoughts unfolded before him like real scenes. With his eyes fixed on darkness, he saw. When at the end of his journey through the streets, after entering the arcade, and climbing the little staircase, he thought he perceived Therese, ardent and pale, he briskly sprang from his bed, murmuring:

"I must go there. She's waiting for me."

This abrupt movement drove away the hallucination. He felt the chill of the tile flooring, and was afraid. For a moment he stood motionless on his bare feet, listening. He fancied he heard a sound on the landing. And he reflected that if he went to Therese, he would again have to pass before the door of the cellar below. This thought sent a cold shiver down his back. Again he was seized with fright, a sort of stupid crushing terror. He looked distrustfully round the room, where he distinguished shreds of whitish light. Then gently, with anxious, hasty precautions, he went to bed again, and there huddling himself together, hid himself, as if to escape a weapon, a knife that threatened him.

The blood had flown violently to his neck, which was burning him. He put his hand there, and beneath his fingers felt the scar of the bite he had received from Camille. He had almost forgotten this wound and was terrified when he found it on his skin, where it seemed to be gnawing into his flesh. He rapidly withdrew his hand so as not to feel the scar, but he was still conscious of its being there boring into and devouring his neck. Then, when he delicately scratched it with his nail, the terrible burning sensation increased twofold. So as not to tear the skin, he pressed his two hands between his doubled-up knees, and he remained thus, rigid and irritated, with the gnawing pain in his neck, and his teeth chattering with fright.

His mind now settled on Camille with frightful tenacity. Hitherto the drowned man had not troubled him at night. And behold the thought of Therese brought up the spectre of her husband. The murderer dared not open his eyes, afraid of perceiving his victim in a corner of the room. At one moment, he fancied his bedstead was being shaken in a peculiar manner. He imagined Camille was beneath it, and that it was he who was tossing him about in this way so as to make him fall and bite him. With haggard look and hair on end, he clung to his mattress, imagining the jerks were becoming more and more violent.

Then, he perceived the bed was not moving, and he felt a reaction. He sat up, lit his candle, and taxed himself with being an idiot. He next swallowed a large glassful of water to appease his fever.

"I was wrong to drink at that wine-shop," thought he. "I don't know what is the matter with me to-night. It's silly. I shall be worn out to-morrow at my office. I ought to have gone to sleep at once, when I got into bed, instead of thinking of a lot of things. That is what gave me insomnia. I must get to sleep at once."

Again he blew out the light. He buried his head in the pillow, feeling slightly refreshed, and thoroughly determined not to think any more, and to be no more afraid. Fatigue began to relax his nerves.

He did not fall into his usual heavy, crushing sleep, but glided lightly into unsettled slumber. He simply felt as if benumbed, as if plunged into gentle and delightful stupor. As he dozed, he could feel his limbs. His intelligence remained awake in his deadened frame. He had driven away his thoughts, he had resisted the vigil. Then, when he became appeased, when his strength failed and his will escaped him, his thoughts returned quietly, one by one, regaining possession of his faltering being.

His reverie began once more. Again he went over the distance separating him from Therese: he went downstairs, he passed before the cellar at a run, and found himself outside the house; he took all the streets he had followed before, when he was dreaming with his eyes open; he entered the Arcade of the Pont Neuf, ascended the little staircase and scratched at the door. But instead of Therese, it was Camille who opened the door, Camille, just as he had seen him at the Morgue, looking greenish, and atrociously disfigured. The corpse extended his arms to him, with a vile laugh, displaying the tip of a blackish tongue between its white teeth.

Laurent shrieked, and awoke with a start. He was bathed in perspiration. He pulled the bedclothes over his eyes, swearing and getting into a rage with himself. He wanted to go to sleep again. And he did so as before, slowly.

The same feeling of heaviness overcame him, and as soon as his will had again escaped in the languidness of semi-slumber, he set out again. He returned where his fixed idea conducted him; he ran to see Therese, and once more it was the drowned man who opened the door.

The wretch sat up terrified. He would have given anything in the world to be able to drive away this implacable dream. He longed for heavy sleep to crush his thoughts. So long as he remained awake, he had sufficient energy to expel the phantom of his victim; but as soon as he lost command of his mind it led him to the acme of terror.

He again attempted to sleep. Then came a succession of delicious spells of drowsiness, and abrupt, harrowing awakenings. In his furious obstinacy, he still went to Therese, but only to always run against the body of Camille. He performed the same journey more than ten times over. He started all afire, followed the same itinerary, experienced the same sensations, accomplished the same acts, with minute exactitude; and more than ten times over, he saw the drowned man present himself to be embraced, when he extended his arms to seize and clasp his love.

This same sinister catastrophe which awoke him on each occasion, gasping and distracted, did not discourage him. After an interval of a few minutes, as soon as he had fallen asleep again, forgetful of the hideous corpse awaiting him, he once more hurried away to seek the young woman.

Laurent passed an hour a prey to these successive nightmares, to these bad dreams that followed one another ceaselessly, without any warning, and he was struck with more acute terror at each start they gave him.

The last of these shocks proved so violent, so painful that he determined to get up, and struggle no longer. Day was breaking. A gleam of dull, grey light was entering at the window in the roof which cut out a pale grey square in the sky.

Laurent slowly dressed himself, with a feeling of sullen irritation, exasperated at having been unable to sleep, exasperated at allowing himself to be caught by a fright which he now regarded as childish. As he drew on this trousers he stretched himself, he rubbed his limbs, he passed his hands over his face, harassed and clouded by a feverish night. And he repeated:

"I ought not to have thought of all that, I should have gone to sleep. Had I done so, I should be fresh and well-disposed now."

Then it occurred to him that if he had been with Therese, she would have prevented him being afraid, and this idea brought him a little calm. At the bottom of his heart he dreaded passing other nights similar to the one he had just gone through.

After splashing some water in his face, he ran the comb through his hair, and this bit of toilet while refreshing his head, drove away the final vestiges of terror. He now reasoned freely, and experienced no other inconvenience from his restless night, than great fatigue in all his limbs.

"I am not a poltroon though," he said to himself as he finished dressing. "I don't care a fig about Camille. It's absurd to think that this poor devil is under my bed. I shall, perhaps, have the same idea, now, every night. I must certainly marry as soon as possible. When Therese has me in her arms, I shall not think much about Camille. She will kiss me on the neck, and I shall cease to feel the atrocious burn that troubles me at present. Let me examine this bite."

He approached his glass, extended his neck and looked. The scar presented a rosy appearance. Then, Laurent, perceiving the marks of the teeth of his victim, experienced a certain emotion. The blood flew to his head, and he now observed a strange phenomenon. The ruby flood rushing to the scar had turned it purple, it became raw and sanguineous, standing out quite red against the fat, white neck. Laurent at the same time felt a sharp pricking sensation, as if needles were being thrust into the wound, and he hurriedly raised the collar of his shirt again.

"Bah!" he exclaimed, "Therese will cure that. A few kisses will suffice. What a fool I am to think of these matters!"

He put on his hat, and went downstairs. He wanted to be in the open air and walk. Passing before the door of the cellar, he smiled. Nevertheless, he made sure of the strength of the hook fastening the door. Outside, on the deserted pavement, he moved along with short steps in the fresh matutinal air. It was then about five o'clock.

Laurent passed an atrocious day. He had to struggle against the overpowering drowsiness that settled on him in the afternoon at his office. His heavy, aching head nodded in spite of himself, but he abruptly brought it up, as soon as he heard the step of one of his chiefs. This struggle, these shocks completed wearing out his limbs, while causing him intolerable anxiety.

In the evening, notwithstanding his lassitude, he went to see Therese, only to find her feverish, extremely low-spirited, and as weary as himself.

"Our poor Therese has had a bad night," Madame Raquin said to him, as soon as he had seated himself. "It seems she was suffering from nightmare, and terrible insomnia. I heard her crying out on several occasions. This morning she was quite ill."

Therese, while her aunt was speaking, looked fixedly at Laurent. No doubt, they guessed their common terror, for a nervous shudder ran over their countenances. Until ten o'clock they remained face to face with one another, talking of commonplace matters, but still understanding each other, and mutually imploring themselves with their eyes, to hasten the moment when they could unite against the drowned man.

CHAPTER XVIII

Therese also had been visited by the spectre of Camille, during this feverish night.

After over a year of indifference, Laurent's sudden attentions had aroused her senses. As she tossed herself about in insomnia, she had seen the drowned man rise up before her; like Laurent she had writhed in terror, and she had said as he had done, that she would no longer be afraid, that she would no more experience such sufferings, when she had her sweetheart in her arms.

This man and woman had experienced at the same hour, a sort of nervous disorder which set them panting with terror. A consanguinity had become established between them. They shuddered with the same shudder; their hearts in a kind of poignant friendship, were wrung with the same anguish. From that moment they had one body and one soul for enjoyment and suffering.

This communion, this mutual penetration is a psychological and physiological phenomenon which is often found to exist in beings who have been brought into violent contact by great nervous shocks.

For over a year, Therese and Laurent lightly bore the chain riveted to their limbs that united them. In the depression succeeding the acute crisis of the murder, amidst the feelings of disgust, and the need for calm and oblivion that had followed, these two convicts might fancy they were free, that they were no longer shackled together by iron fetters. The slackened chain dragged on the ground. They reposed, they found themselves struck with a sort of delightful insensibility, they sought to love elsewhere, to live in a state of wise equilibrium. But from the day when urged forward by events, they came to the point of again exchanging burning sentences, the chain became violently strained, and they received such a shock, that they felt themselves for ever linked to one another.

The day following this first attack of nightmare, Therese secretly set to work to bring about her marriage with Laurent. It was a difficult task, full of peril. The sweethearts trembled lest they should commit an imprudence, arouse suspicions, and too abruptly reveal the interest they had in the death of Camille.

Convinced that they could not mention marriage themselves, they arranged a very clever plan which consisted in getting Madame Raquin herself, and the Thursday evening guests, to offer them what they dared not ask for. It then only became necessary to convey to these worthy people the idea of remarrying Therese, and particularly to make them believe that this idea originated with themselves, and was their own.

The comedy was long and delicate to perform. Therese and Laurent took the parts adapted to them, and proceeded with extreme prudence, calculating the slightest gesture, and the least word. At the bottom of their hearts, they were devoured by a feeling of impatience that stiffened and strained their nerves. They lived in a state of constant irritation, and it required all their natural cowardice to compel them to show a smiling and peaceful exterior.

If they yearned to bring the business to an end, it was because they could no longer remain separate and solitary. Each night, the drowned man visited them, insomnia stretched them on beds of live coal and turned them over with fiery tongs. The state of enervation in which they lived, nightly increased the fever of their blood, which resulted in atrocious hallucinations rising up before them.

Therese no longer dared enter her room after dusk. She experienced the keenest anguish, when she had to shut herself until morning in this large apartment, which became lit-up with strange glimmers, and peopled with phantoms as soon as the light was out. She ended by leaving her candle burning, and by preventing herself falling asleep, so as to always have her eyes wide open. But when fatigue lowered her lids, she saw Camille in the dark, and reopened her eyes with a start. In the morning she dragged herself about, broken down, having only slumbered for a few hours at dawn.

As to Laurent, he had decidedly become a poltroon since the night he had taken fright when passing before the cellar door. Previous to that incident he had lived with the confidence of a brute; now, at the least sound, he trembled and turned pale like a little boy. A shudder of terror had suddenly shaken his limbs, and had clung to him. At night, he suffered even more than Therese; and fright, in this great, soft, cowardly frame, produced profound laceration to the feelings. He watched the fall of day with cruel apprehension. On several occasions, he failed to return home, and passed whole nights walking in the middle of the deserted streets.

Once he remained beneath a bridge, until morning, while the rain poured down in torrents; and there, huddled up, half frozen, not daring to rise and ascend to the quay, he for nearly six hours watched the dirty water running in the whitish shadow. At times a fit of terror brought him flat down on the damp ground: under one of the arches of the bridge he seemed to see long lines of drowned bodies drifting along in the current. When weariness drove him home, he shut himself in, and double-locked the door. There he struggled until daybreak amidst frightful attacks of fever.

The same nightmare returned persistently: he fancied he fell from the ardent clasp of Therese into the cold, sticky arms of Camille. He dreamt, first of all, that his sweetheart was stifling him in a warm embrace, and then that the corpse of the drowned man pressed him to his chest in an ice-like strain. These abrupt and alternate sensations of voluptuousness and disgust, these successive contacts of burning love and frigid death, set him panting for breath, and caused him to shudder and gasp in anguish.

Each day, the terror of the lovers increased, each day their attacks of nightmare crushed and maddened them the more. They no longer relied on their kisses to drive away insomnia. By prudence, they did not dare make appointments, but looked forward to their wedding-day as a day of salvation, to be followed by an untroubled night.

It was their desire for calm slumber that made them wish for their union. They had hesitated during the hours of indifference, both being oblivious of the egotistic and impassioned reasons that had urged them to the crime, and which were now dispelled. It was in vague despair that they took the supreme resolution to unite openly. At the bottom of their hearts they were afraid. They had leant, so to say, one on the other above an unfathomable depth, attracted to it by its horror. They bent over the abyss together, clinging silently to one another, while feelings of intense giddiness enfeebled their limbs and gave them falling madness.

But at the present moment, face to face with their anxious expectation and timorous desires, they felt the imperative necessity of closing their eyes, and of dreaming of a future full of amorous felicity and peaceful enjoyment. The more they trembled one before the other, the better they foresaw the horror of the abyss to the bottom of which they were about to plunge, and the more they sought to make promises of happiness to themselves, and to spread out before their eyes the invincible facts that fatally led them to marriage.

Therese desired her union with Laurent solely because she was afraid and wanted a companion. She was a prey to nervous attacks that drove her half crazy. In reality she reasoned but little, she flung herself into love with a mind upset by the novels she had recently been reading, and a frame irritated by the cruel insomnia that had kept her awake for several weeks.

Laurent, who was of a stouter constitution, while giving way to his terror and his desire, had made up his mind to reason out his decision. To thoroughly prove to himself that his marriage was necessary, that he was at last going to be perfectly happy, and to drive away the vague fears that beset him, he resumed all his former calculations.

His father, the peasant of Jeufosse, seemed determined not to die, and Laurent said to himself that he might have to wait a long time for the inheritance. He even feared that this inheritance might escape him, and go into the pockets of one of his cousins, a great big fellow who turned the soil over to the keen satisfaction of the old boy. And he would remain poor; he would live the life of a bachelor in a garret, with a bad bed and a worse table. Besides, he did not contemplate working all his life; already he began to find his office singularly tedious. The light labour entrusted to him became irksome owing to his laziness.

The invariable result of these reflections was that supreme happiness consisted in doing nothing. Then he remembered that if he had drowned Camille, it was to marry Therese, and work no more. Certainly, the thought of having his sweetheart all to himself had greatly influenced him in committing the crime, but he had perhaps been led to it still more, by the hope of taking the place of Camille, of being looked after in the same way, and of enjoying constant beatitude. Had passion alone urged him to the deed, he would not have shown such cowardice and prudence. The truth was that he had sought by murder to assure himself a calm, indolent life, and the satisfaction of his cravings.

All these thoughts, avowedly or unconsciously, returned to him. To find encouragement, he repeated that it was time to gather in the harvest anticipated by the death of Camille, and he spread out before him, the advantages and blessings of his future existence: he would leave his office, and live in delicious idleness; he would eat, drink and sleep to his heart's content; he would have an affectionate wife beside him; and, he would shortly inherit the 40,000 francs and more of Madame Raquin, for the poor old woman was dying, little by little, every day; in a word, he would carve out for himself the existence of a happy brute, and would forget everything.

Laurent mentally repeated these ideas at every moment, since his marriage with Therese had been decided on. He also sought other advantages that would result therefrom, and felt delighted when he found a new argument, drawn from his egotism, in favour of his union with the widow of the drowned man. But however much he forced himself to hope, however much he dreamed of a future full of idleness and pleasure, he never ceased to feel abrupt shudders that gave his skin an icy chill, while at moments he continued to experience an anxiety that stifled his joy in his throat.

CHAPTER XIX

In the meanwhile, the secret work of Therese and Laurent was productive of results. The former had assumed a woeful and despairing demeanour which at the end of a few days alarmed Madame Raquin. When the old mercer inquired what made her niece so sad, the young woman played the part of an inconsolable widow with consummate skill. She spoke in a vague manner of feeling weary, depressed, of suffering from her nerves, without making any precise complaint. When pressed by her aunt with questions, she replied that she was well, that she could not imagine what it was that made her so low-spirited, and that she shed tears without knowing why.

Then, the constant choking fits of sobbing, the wan, heartrending smiles, the spells of crushing silence full of emptiness and despair, continued.

The sight of this young woman who was always giving way to her grief, who seemed to be slowly dying of some unknown complaint, ended by seriously alarming Madame Raquin. She had, now, no one in the whole world but her niece, and she prayed the Almighty every night to preserve her this relative to close her eyes. A little egotism was mingled with this final love of her old age. She felt herself affected in the slight consolations that still assisted her to live, when it crossed her mind that she might die alone in the damp shop in the arcade. From that time, she never took her eyes off her niece, and it was with terror that she watched her sadness, wondering what she could do to cure her of her silent despair.

Under these grave circumstances, she thought she ought to take the advice of her old friend Michaud. One Thursday evening, she detained him in the shop, and spoke to him of her alarm.

"Of course," answered the old man, with that frank brutality he had acquired in the performance of his former functions, "I have noticed for some time past that Therese has been looking sour, and I know very well why her face is quite yellow and overspread with grief."

"You know why!" exclaimed the widow. "Speak out at once. If we could only cure her!"

"Oh! the treatment is simple," resumed Michaud with a laugh. "Your niece finds life irksome because she had been alone for nearly two years. She wants a husband; you can see that in her eyes."

The brutal frankness of the former commissary, gave Madame Raquin a painful shock. She fancied that the wound Therese had received through the fatal accident at Saint-Ouen, was still as fresh, still as cruel at the bottom of her heart. It seemed to her that her son, once dead, Therese could have no thought for a husband, and here was Michaud affirming, with a hearty laugh, that Therese was out of sorts because she wanted one.

"Marry her as soon as you can," said he, as he took himself off, "if you do not wish to see her shrivel up entirely. That is my advice, my dear lady, and it is good, believe me."

Madame Raquin could not, at first, accustom herself to the thought that her son was already forgotten. Old Michaud had not even pronounced the name of Camille, and had made a joke of the pretended illness of Therese. The poor mother understood that she alone preserved at the bottom of her heart, the living recollection of her dear child, and she wept, for it seemed to her that Camille had just died a second time.

Then, when she had had a good cry, and was weary of mourning, she thought, in spite of herself, of what Michaud had said, and became familiar with the idea of purchasing a little happiness at the cost of a marriage which, according to her delicate mind, was like killing her son again.

Frequently, she gave way to feelings of cowardice when she came face to face with the dejected and broken-down Therese, amidst the icy silence of the shop. She was not one of those dry, rigid persons who find bitter delight in living a life of eternal despair. Her character was full of pliancy, devotedness, and effusion, which contributed to make up her temperament of a stout and affable good lady, and prompted her to live in a state of active tenderness.

Since her niece no longer spoke, and remained there pale and feeble, her own life became intolerable, while the shop seemed to her like a tomb. What she required was to find some warm affection beside her, some liveliness, some caresses, something sweet and gay which would help her to wait peacefully for death. It was these unconscious desires that made her accept the idea of marrying Therese again; she even forgot her son a little. In the existence of the tomb that she was leading, came a sort of awakening, something like a will, and fresh occupation for the mind. She sought a husband for her niece, and this search gave her matter for consideration.

The choice of a husband was an important business. The poor old lady thought much more of her own comfort than of Therese. She wished to marry her niece in order to be happy herself, for she had keen misgivings lest the new husband of the young woman should come and trouble the last hours of her old age. The idea that she was about to introduce a stranger into her daily existence terrified her. It was this thought alone that stopped her, that prevented her from talking openly with her niece about matrimony.

While Therese acted the comedy of weariness and dejection with that perfect hypocrisy she had acquired by her education, Laurent took the part of a sensible and serviceable man. He was full of little attentions for the two women, particularly for Madame Raquin, whom he overwhelmed with delicate attention. Little by little he made himself indispensable in the shop; it was him alone who brought a little gaiety into this black hole. When he did not happen to be there of an evening, the old mercer searched round her, ill at ease, as if she missed something, being almost afraid to find herself face to face with the despairing Therese.

But Laurent only occasionally absented himself to better prove his power. He went to the shop daily, on quitting his office, and remained there until the arcade was closed at night. He ran the errands, and handed Madame Raquin, who could only walk with difficulty, the small articles she required. Then he seated himself and chatted. He had acquired the gentle penetrating voice of an actor which he employed to flatter the ears and heart of the good old lady. In a friendly way, he seemed particularly anxious about the health of Therese, like a tender-hearted man who feels for the sufferings of others. On repeated occasions, he took Madame Raquin to one side, and terrified her by appearing very much alarmed himself at the changes and ravages he said he perceived on the face of the young woman.

"We shall soon lose her," he murmured in a tearful voice. "We cannot conceal from ourselves that she is extremely ill. Ah! alas, for our poor happiness, and our nice tranquil evenings!"

Madame Raquin listened to him with anguish. Laurent even had the audacity to speak of Camille.

"You see," said he to the mercer, "the death of my poor friend has been a terrible blow to her. She had been dying for the last two years, since that fatal day when she lost Camille. Nothing will console her, nothing will cure her. We must be resigned."

These impudent falsehoods made the old lady shed bitter tears. The memory of her son troubled and blinded her. Each time the name of Camille was pronounced, she gave way, bursting into sobs. She would have embraced the person who mentioned her poor boy. Laurent had noticed the trouble, and outburst of tender feeling that this name produced. He could make her weep at will, upset her with such emotion that she failed to distinguish the clear aspect of things; and he took advantage of this power to always hold her pliant and in pain in his hand, as it were.

Each evening in spite of the secret revolt of his trembling inner being, he brought the conversation to bear on the rare qualities, on the tender heart and mind of Camille, praising his victim with most shameless impudence. At moments, when he found the eyes of Therese fixed with a strange expression on his own, he shuddered, and ended by believing all the good he had been saying about the drowned man. Then he held his tongue, suddenly seized with atrocious jealousy, fearing that the young widow loved the man he had flung into the water, and whom he now lauded with the conviction of an enthusiast.

Throughout the conversation Madame Raquin was in tears, and unable to distinguish anything around her. As she wept, she reflected that Laurent must have a loving and generous heart. He alone remembered her son, he alone still spoke of him in a trembling and affected voice. She dried her eyes, gazing at the young man with infinite tenderness, and feeling that she loved him as her own child.

One Thursday evening, Michaud and Grivet were already in the dining-room, when Laurent coming in, approached Therese, and with gentle anxiety inquired after her health. He seated himself for a moment beside her, performing for the edification of the persons present, his part of an alarmed and affectionate friend. As the young couple sat close together, exchanging a few words, Michaud, who was observing them, bent down, and said in a low voice to the old mercer, as he pointed to Laurent:

"Look, there is the husband who will suit your niece. Arrange this marriage quickly. We will assist you if it be necessary."

This remark came as a revelation to Madame Raquin. She saw, at once, all the advantages she would derive, personally, from the union of

Therese and Laurent. The marriage would tighten the bonds already connecting her and her niece with the friend of her son, with that good-natured fellow who came to amuse them in the evening.

In this manner, she would not be introducing a stranger into her home, she would not run the risk of unhappiness. On the contrary, while giving Therese a support, she added another joy to her old age, she found a second son in this young man who for three years had shown her such filial affection.

Then it occurred to her that Therese would be less faithless to the memory of Camille by marrying Laurent. The religion of the heart is peculiarly delicate. Madame Raquin, who would have wept to see a stranger embrace the young widow, felt no repulsion at the thought of giving her to the comrade of her son.

Throughout the evening, while the guests played at dominoes, the old mercer watched the couple so tenderly, that they guessed the comedy had succeeded, and that the denouement was at hand. Michaud, before withdrawing, had a short conversation in an undertone with Madame Raquin. Then, he pointedly took the arm of Laurent saying he would accompany him a bit of the way. As Laurent went off, he exchanged a rapid glance with Therese, a glance full of urgent enjoinment.

Michaud had undertaken to feel the ground. He found the young man very much devoted to the two ladies, but exceedingly astonished at the idea of a marriage between Therese and himself. Laurent added, in an unsteady tone of voice, that he loved the widow of his poor friend as a sister, and that it would seem to him a perfect sacrilege to marry her. The former commissary of police insisted, giving numerous good reasons with a view to obtaining his consent. He even spoke of devotedness, and went so far as to tell the young man that it was clearly his duty to give a son to Madame Raquin and a husband to Therese.

Little by little Laurent allowed himself to be won over, feigning to give way to emotion, to accept the idea of this marriage as one fallen from the clouds, dictated by feelings of devotedness and duty, as old Michaud had said. When the latter had obtained a formal answer in the affirmative, he parted with his companion, rubbing his hands, for he fancied he had just gained a great victory. He prided himself on having had the first idea of this marriage which would convey to the Thursday evenings all their former gaiety.

While Michaud was talking with Laurent, slowly following the quays, Madame Raquin had an almost identical conversation with Therese. At the moment when her niece, pale and unsteady in gait, as usual, was about to retire to rest, the old mercer detained her an instant. She questioned her in a tender tone, imploring her to be frank, and confess the cause of the trouble that overwhelmed her. Then, as she only obtained vague replies, she spoke of the emptiness of widowhood, and little by little came to talk in a more precise manner of the offer of a second marriage, concluding by asking Therese, plainly, whether she had not a secret desire to marry again.

Therese protested, saying that such a thought had never entered her mind, and that she intended remaining faithful to Camille. Madame Raquin began to weep. Pleading against her heart, she gave her niece to understand that despair should not be eternal; and, finally, in response to an exclamation of the young woman saying she would never replace Camille, Madame Raquin abruptly pronounced the name of Laurent. Then she enlarged with a flood of words on the propriety and advantages of such an union. She poured out her mind, repeating aloud all she had been thinking during the evening, depicting with naive egotism, the picture of her final days of happiness, between her two dear children. Therese, resigned and docile, listened to her with bowed head, ready to give satisfaction to her slightest wish.

"I love Laurent as a brother," said she grievously, when her aunt had ceased speaking. "But, as you desire it, I will endeavour to love him as a husband. I wish to make you happy. I had hoped that you would have allowed me to weep in peace, but I will dry my tears, as it is a question of your happiness."

She kissed the old lady, who remained surprised and frightened at having been the first to forget her son. As Madame Raquin went to bed, she sobbed bitterly, accusing herself of having less strength than Therese, and of desiring, out of egotism, a marriage that the young widow accepted by simple abnegation.

The following morning, Michaud and his old friend had a short conversation in the arcade, before the door of the shop, where they communicated to one another the result of their efforts, and agreed to hurry matters on by forcing the young people to become affianced the same evening.

At five o'clock, Michaud was already in the shop when Laurent entered. As soon as the young man had seated himself, the former commissary of police said in his ear:

"She accepts."

This blunt remark was overheard by Therese who remained pale, with her eyes impudently fixed on Laurent. The two sweethearts looked at each other for a few seconds as if consulting. Both understood that they must accept the position without hesitation, and finish the business at one stroke. Laurent, rising, went and took the hand of Madame Raquin, who made every effort to restrain her tears.

"Dear mother," said he smiling, "I was talking about your felicity, last night, with M. Michaud. Your children wish to make you happy."

The poor old lady, on hearing herself called "dear mother," allowed her tears to flow. She quietly seized the hand of Therese and placed it in that of Laurent, unable to utter a single word.

The two sweethearts shivered on feeling their skins touch, and remained with their burning fingers pressed together, in a nervous clasp. After a pause, the young man, in a hesitating tone, resumed:

"Therese, shall we give your aunt a bright and peaceful existence?"

"Yes," feebly replied the young woman, "we have a duty to perform."

Then Laurent, becoming very pale, turned towards Madame Raquin, and added:

"When Camille fell into the water, he shouted out to me: 'Save my wife, I entrust her to you.' I believe I am acting in accordance with his last wish in marrying Therese."

Therese, on hearing these words, let go the hand of Laurent. She had received a shock like a blow in the chest. The impudence of her sweetheart overwhelmed her. She observed him with a senseless look, while Madame Raquin, half stifled by sobs, stammered:

"Yes, yes, my friend, marry her, make her happy; my son, from the depth of his tomb, will thank you."

Laurent, feeling himself giving way, leant on the back of a chair, while Michaud, who was himself moved to tears, pushed him towards Therese with the remark:

"Kiss one another. It will be your betrothal."

When the lips of the young man came in contact with the cheeks of the widow, he experienced a peculiarly uncomfortable feeling, while the latter abruptly drew back, as if the two kisses of her sweetheart burnt her. This was the first caress he had given her in the presence of witnesses. All her blood rushed to her face, and she felt herself red and burning.

After this crisis, the two murderers breathed. Their marriage was decided on. At last they approached the goal they had so long had in view. Everything was settled the same evening. The Thursday following, the marriage was announced to Grivet, as well as to Olivier and his wife. Michaud, in communicating the news to them, did not conceal his delight. He rubbed his hands, repeating as he did so:

"It was I who thought of it. It is I who have married them. You will see what a nice couple they'll make!"

Suzanne silently embraced Therese. This poor creature, who was half dead, and as white as a sheet, had formed a friendship for the rigid and sombre young widow. She showed her a sort of childlike affection mingled with a kind of respectful terror. Olivier complimented the aunt and niece, while Grivet hazarded a few spicy jokes that met with middling success. Altogether the company were delighted, enchanted, and declared that everything was for the best; in reality all they thought about was the wedding feast.

Therese and Laurent were clever enough to maintain a suitable demeanour, by simply displaying tender and obliging friendship to one another. They gave themselves an air of accomplishing an act of supreme devotedness. Nothing in their faces betrayed a suspicion of the terror and desire that disturbed them. Madame Raquin watched the couple with faint smiles, and a look of feeble, but grateful goodwill.

A few formalities required fulfilling. Laurent had to write to his father to ask his consent to the marriage. The old peasant of Jeufosse who had almost forgotten that he had a son at Paris, answered him, in four lines, that he could marry, and go and get hanged if he chose. He gave him to understand that being resolved never to give him a sou, he left him master of his body, and authorised him to be guilty of all imaginable follies. A permission accorded in such terms, caused Laurent singular anxiety.

Madame Raquin, after reading the letter of this unnatural father, in a transport of kind-heartedness, acted very foolishly. She made over to her niece the 40,000 francs and more, that she possessed, stripping herself entirely for the young couple, on whose affection she relied, with the desire of being indebted to them for all her happiness.

Laurent brought nothing into the community, and he even gave it to be understood that he did not always intend to remain in his present employment, but would perhaps take up painting again. In any case, the future of the little family was assured; the interest on the money put aside added to the profit on the mercery business, would be sufficient to keep three persons comfortably. As a matter of fact it was only just sufficient to make them happy.

The preparations for the marriage were hurried on, the formalities being abridged as much as possible, and at last the welcome day arrived.

CHAPTER XX

In the morning, Laurent and Therese, awoke in their respective rooms, with the same feeling of profound joy in their hearts: both said to themselves that their last night of terror had passed. They would no longer have to sleep alone, and they would mutually defend themselves against the drowned man.

Therese looked around her, giving a strange smile as she measured her great bed with her eyes. She rose and began to slowly dress herself, in anticipation of the arrival of Suzanne, who was to come and assist her with her bridal toilet.

Laurent, on awakening, sat up in bed, and remained in that position for a few minutes, bidding farewell to his garret, which struck him as vile. At last he was to quit this kennel and have a wife. It was in the month of December and he shivered. He sprang on the tile floor, saying to himself that he would be warm at night.

A week previously, Madame Raquin, knowing how short he was of money, had slipped a purse into his hand containing 500 francs, which represented all her savings. The young man had accepted this present without difficulty, and had rigged himself out from tip to toe. Moreover, the money of the old mercer permitted him to make Therese the customary presents.

The black trousers, dress coat, white waistcoat, shirt and cambric tie, hung spread out on a couple of chairs. Laurent washed, perfumed himself with a bottle of eau de Cologne, and then proceeded to carefully attire himself. He wished to look handsome. As he fastened his collar, a collar which was high and stiff, he experienced keen pain in the neck. The button escaped from his fingers. He lost patience. The starched linen seemed to cut into his flesh. Wishing to see what was the matter, he raised his chin, and perceived the bite Camille had given him looking quite red. The collar had slightly galled the scar.

Laurent pressed his lips together, and turned pale; the sight of this mark seaming his neck, frightened and irritated him at this moment. He crumpled up the collar, and selected another which he put on with every precaution, and then finished dressing himself. As he went downstairs his new clothes made him look rigid. With his neck imprisoned in the inflexible linen, he dared not turn his head. At every movement he made, a pleat pinched the wound that the teeth of the drowned man had made in his flesh, and it was under the irritation of these sharp pricks, that he got into the carriage, and went to fetch Therese to conduct her to the town-hall and church.

On the way, he picked up a clerk employed at the Orleans Railway Company, and old Michaud, who were to act as witnesses. When they reached the shop, everyone was ready: Grivet and Olivier, the witnesses of Therese, were there, along with Suzanne, who looked at the bride as little girls look at dolls they have just dressed up. Although Madame Raquin was no longer able to walk, she desired to accompany the couple everywhere, so she was hoisted into a conveyance and the party set out.

Everything passed off in a satisfactory manner at the town-hall and church. The calm and modest attitude of the bride and bridegroom was remarked and approved. They pronounced the sacramental "yes" with an emotion that moved Grivet himself. They were as if in a dream. Whether seated, or quietly kneeling side by side, they were rent by raging thoughts that flashed through their minds in spite of themselves, and they avoided looking at one another. When they seated themselves in their carriage, they seemed to be greater strangers than before.

It had been decided that the wedding feast should be a family affair at a little restaurant on the heights of Belleville. The Michauds and Grivet alone were invited. Until six in the evening, the wedding party drove along the boulevards, and then repaired to the cheap eating-house where a table was spread with seven covers in a small private room painted yellow, and reeking of dust and wine.

The repast was not accompanied by much gaiety. The newly married pair were grave and thoughtful. Since the morning, they had been experiencing strange sensations, which they did not seek to fathom. From the commencement, they had felt bewildered at the rapidity with which the formalities and ceremony were performed, that had just bound them together for ever.

Then, the long drive on the boulevards had soothed them and made them drowsy. It appeared to them that this drive lasted months. Nevertheless, they allowed themselves to be taken through the monotonous streets without displaying impatience, looking at the shops and people with sparkless eyes, overcome by a numbness that made them feel stupid, and which they endeavoured to shake off by bursting into fits of laughter. When they entered the restaurant, they were weighed down by oppressive fatigue, while increasing stupor continued to settle on them.

Placed at table opposite one another, they smiled with an air of constraint, and then fell into the same heavy reverie as before, eating, answering questions, moving their limbs like machines. Amidst the idle lassitude of their minds, the same string of flying thoughts returned ceaselessly. They were married, and yet unconscious of their new condition, which caused them profound astonishment. They imagined an abyss still separated them, and at moments asked themselves how they could get over this unfathomable depth. They fancied they were living previous to the murder, when a material obstacle stood between them.

Then they abruptly remembered they would occupy the same apartment that night, in a few hours, and they gazed at one another in astonishment, unable to comprehend why they should be permitted to do so. They did not feel they were united, but, on the contrary, were dreaming that they had just been violently separated, and one cast far from the other.

The silly chuckling of the guests beside them, who wished to hear them talk familiarly, so as to dispel all restraint, made them stammer and colour. They could never make up their minds to treat one another as sweethearts in the presence of company.

Waiting had extinguished the flame that had formerly fired them. All the past had disappeared. They had forgotten their violent passion, they forgot even their joy of the morning, that profound joy they had experienced at the thought that they would no more be afraid. They were simply wearied and bewildered at all that was taking place. The events of the day turned round and round in their heads, appearing incomprehensible and monstrous. They sat there mute and smiling, expecting nothing, hoping for nothing. Mingled with their dejection of spirits, was a restless anxiety that proved vaguely painful.

At every movement Laurent made with his neck, he felt a sharp burn devouring his flesh; his collar cut and pinched the bite of Camille. While the mayor read out to him the law bearing on marriage, while the priest spoke to him of the Almighty, at every minute of this long day, he had felt the teeth of the drowned man entering his skin. At times, he imagined a streak of blood was running down his chest, and would bespatter his white waistcoat with crimson.

Madame Raquin was inwardly grateful to the newly married couple for their gravity. Noisy joy would have wounded the poor mother. In her mind, her son was there, invisible, handing Therese over to Laurent.

Grivet had other ideas. He considered the wedding party sad, and wanted to enliven it, notwithstanding the looks of Michaud and Olivier which riveted him to his chair each time he wished to get up and say something silly. Nevertheless, he managed to rise once and propose a toast.

"I drink to the offspring of monsieur and madame," quoth he in a sprightly tone.

It was necessary to touch glasses. Therese and Laurent had turned extremely pale on hearing this sentence. They had never dreamed that they might have children. The thought flashed through them like an icy shiver. They nervously joined glasses with the others, examining one another, surprised and alarmed to find themselves there, face to face.

The party rose from table early. The guests wished to accompany the newly married pair to the nuptial chamber. It was barely half-past nine when they all returned to the shop in the arcade. The dealer in imitation jewelry was still there in her cupboard, before the box lined with blue velvet. She raised her head inquisitively, gazing at the young husband and wife with a smile. The latter caught her eyes, and was terrified. It struck her that perhaps this old woman was aware of their former meetings, by having noticed Laurent slipping into the little corridor.

When they all arrived on the upper floor, Therese withdrew almost immediately, with Madame Raquin and Suzanne, the men remaining in the dining-room, while the bride performed her toilet for the night. Laurent, nerveless and depressed, did not experience the least impatience, but listened complacently to the coarse jokes of old Michaud and Grivet, who indulged themselves to their hearts' content, now that the ladies were no longer present. When Suzanne and Madame Raquin quitted the nuptial apartment, and the old mercer in an unsteady voice told the young man that his wife awaited him, he started. For an instant he remained bewildered. Then he feverishly grasped the hands extended to him, and entered the room, clinging to the door like a man under the influence of drink.

CHAPTER XXI

Laurent carefully closed the door behind him, and for a moment or two stood leaning against it, gazing round the apartment in anxiety and embarrassment.

A clear fire burned on the hearth, sending large sheets of light dancing on ceiling and walls. The room was thus lit-up by bright vacillating gleams, that in a measure annulled the effects of the lamp placed on a table in their midst. Madame Raquin had done her best to convey a coquettish aspect to the apartment. It was one mass of white, and perfumed throughout, as if to serve as a nest for young, fresh love. The good lady, moreover, had taken pleasure in adding a few bits of lace to the bed, and in filling the vases on the chimney-piece with bunches of roses. Gentle warmth and pleasant fragrance reigned over all, and not a sound broke the silence, save the crackling and little sharp reports of the wood aglow on the hearth.

Therese was seated on a low chair to the right of the chimney, staring fixedly at the bright flames, with her chin in her hand. She did not turn her head when Laurent entered. Clothed in a petticoat and linen night-jacket bordered with lace, she looked snowy white in the bright light of the fire. Her jacket had become disarranged, and part of her rosy shoulder appeared, half hidden by a tress of raven hair.

Laurent advanced a few paces without speaking, and took off his coat and waistcoat. When he stood in his shirt sleeves, he again looked at Therese, who had not moved, and he seemed to hesitate. Then, perceiving the bit of shoulder, he bent down quivering, to press his lips to it. The young woman, abruptly turning round, withdrew her shoulder, and in doing so, fixed on Laurent such a strange look of repugnance and horror, that he shrank back, troubled and ill at ease, as if himself seized with terror and disgust.

Laurent then seated himself opposite Therese, on the other side of the chimney, and they remained thus, silent and motionless, for fully five minutes. At times, tongues of reddish flame escaped from the wood, and then the faces of the murderers were touched with fleeting gleams of blood.

It was more than a couple of years since the two sweethearts had found themselves shut up alone in this room. They had arranged no love-meetings since the day when Therese had gone to the Rue Saint-Victor to convey to Laurent the idea of murder. Prudence had kept them apart. Barely had they, at long intervals, ventured on a pressure of the hand, or a stealthy kiss. After the murder of Camille, they had restrained their passion, awaiting the nuptial night. This had at last arrived, and now they remained anxiously face to face, overcome with sudden discomfort.

They had but to stretch forth their arms to clasp one another in a passionate embrace, and their arms remained lifeless, as if worn out with fatigue. The depression they had experienced during the daytime, now oppressed them more and more. They observed one another with timid embarrassment, pained to remain so silent and cold. Their burning dreams ended in a peculiar reality: it sufficed that they should have succeeded in killing Camille, and have become married, it sufficed that the lips of Laurent should have grazed the shoulder of Therese, for their lust to be satisfied to the point of disgust and horror.

In despair, they sought to find within them a little of that passion which formerly had devoured them. Their frames seemed deprived of muscles and nerves, and their embarrassment and anxiety increased. They felt ashamed of remaining so silent and gloomy face to face with one another. They would have liked to have had the strength to squeeze each other to death, so as not to pass as idiots in their own eyes.

What! they belonged one to the other, they had killed a man, and played an atrocious comedy in order to be able to love in peace, and they sat there, one on either side of a mantelshelf, rigid, exhausted, their minds disturbed and their frames lifeless! Such a denouement appeared to them horribly and cruelly ridiculous. It was then that Laurent endeavoured to speak of love, to conjure up the remembrances of other days, appealing to his imagination for a revival of his tenderness.

"Therese," he said, "don't you recall our afternoons in this room? Then I came in by that door, but today I came in by this one. We are free now. We can make love in peace."

He spoke in a hesitating, spiritless manner, and the young woman, huddled up on her low chair, continued gazing dreamily at the flame without listening. Laurent went on:

"Remember how I used to dream of staying a whole night with you? I dreamed of waking up in the morning to your kisses, now it can come true."

Therese all at once started as though surprised to hear a voice stammering in her ears. Turning towards Laurent, on whose countenance the fire, at this moment, cast a broad reddish reflection, she gazed at his sanguinary face, and shuddered.

The young man, more troubled and anxious, resumed:

"We have succeeded, Therese; we have broken through all obstacles, and we belong to one another. The future is ours, is it not? A future of tranquil happiness, of satisfied love. Camille is no longer here—"

Laurent ceased speaking. His throat had suddenly become dry, and he was choking, unable to continue. On hearing the name of Camille, Therese received a violent shock. The two murderers contemplated one another, stupefied, pale, and trembling. The yellow gleams of light from the fire continued to dance on ceiling and walls, the soft odour of roses lingered in the air, the crackling of the wood broke the silence with short, sharp reports.

Remembrances were abandoned. The spectre of Camille which had been evoked, came and seated itself between the newly married pair, in front of the flaming fire. Therese and Laurent recognised the cold, damp smell of the drowned man in the warm air they were breathing. They said to themselves that a corpse was there, close to them, and they examined one another without daring to move. Then all the terrible story of their crime was unfolded in their memory. The name of their victim sufficed to fill them with thoughts of the past, to compel them to go through all the anguish of the murder over again. They did not open their lips, but looked at one another, and both at the same time were troubled with the same nightmare, both with their eyes broached the same cruel tale.

This exchange of terrified looks, this mute narration they were about to make to themselves of the murder, caused them keen and intolerable apprehension. The strain on their nerves threatened an attack, they might cry out, perhaps fight. Laurent, to drive away his recollections, violently tore himself from the ecstasy of horror that enthralled him in the gaze of Therese. He took a few strides in the room; he removed his boots and put on slippers; then, returning to his former place, he sat down at the chimney corner, and tried to talk on matters of indifference.

Therese, understanding what he desired, strove to answer his questions. They chatted about the weather, endeavouring to force on a commonplace conversation. Laurent said the room was warm, and Therese replied that, nevertheless, a draught came from under the small door on the staircase, and both turned in that direction with a sudden shudder. The young man hastened to speak about the roses, the fire, about everything he saw before him. The young woman, with an effort, rejoined in monosyllables, so as not to allow the conversation to drop. They had drawn back from one another, and were giving themselves easy airs, endeavouring to forget whom they were, treating one another as strangers brought together by chance.

But, in spite of themselves, by a strange phenomenon, whilst they uttered these empty phrases, they mutually guessed the thoughts concealed in their banal words. Do what they would, they both thought of Camille. Their eyes continued the story of the past. They still maintained by looks a mute discourse, apart from the conversation they held aloud, which ran haphazard. The words they cast here and there had no signification, being disconnected and contradictory; all their intelligence was bent on the silent exchange of their terrifying recollections.

When Laurent spoke of the roses, or of the fire, of one thing or another, Therese was perfectly well aware that he was reminding her of the struggle in the skiff, of the dull fall of Camille; and, when Therese answered yes or no to an insignificant question, Laurent understood that she said she remembered or did not remember a detail of the crime. They charted it in this manner open-heartedly without needing words, while they spoke aloud of other matters.

Moreover, unconscious of the syllables they pronounced, they followed their secret thoughts sentence by sentence; they might abruptly have continued their confidences aloud, without ceasing to understand each other. This sort of divination, this obstinacy of their memory in presenting to themselves without pause, the image of Camille, little by little drove them crazy. They thoroughly well perceived that they guessed the thoughts of one another, and that if they did not hold their tongues, the words would rise of themselves to their mouths, to name the drowned man, and describe the murder. Then they closely pinched their lips and ceased their conversation.

In the overwhelming silence that ensued, the two murderers continued to converse about their victim. It appeared to them that their eyes mutually penetrated their flesh, and buried clear, keen phrases in their bodies. At moments, they fancied they heard themselves speaking aloud. Their senses changed. Sight became a sort of strange and delicate hearing. They so distinctly read their thoughts upon their countenances, that these thoughts took a peculiarly piercing sound that agitated all their organism. They could not have understood one another better, had they shouted in a heartrending voice:

"We have killed Camille, and his corpse is there, extended between us, making our limbs like ice."

And the terrible confidence continued, more manifest, more resounding, in the calm moist air of the room.

Laurent and Therese had commenced the mute narration from the day of their first interview in the shop. Then the recollections had come one by one in order; they had related their hours of love, their moments of hesitation and anger, the terrible incident of the murder. It was then that they pinched their lips, ceasing to talk of one thing and another, in fear lest they should all at once name Camille without desiring to do so.

But their thoughts failing to cease, had then led them into great distress, into the affrighted period of expectancy following the crime. They thus came to think of the corpse of the drowned man extended on a slab at the Morgue. Laurent, by a look, told Therese all the horror he had felt, and the latter, driven to extremities, compelled by a hand of iron to part her lips, abruptly continued the conversation aloud:

"You saw him at the Morgue?" she inquired of Laurent without naming Camille.

Laurent looked as if he expected this question. He had been reading it for a moment on the livid face of the young woman.

"Yes," answered he in a choking voice.

The murderers shivered, and drawing nearer the fire, extended their hands towards the flame as if an icy puff of wind had suddenly passed through the warm room. For an instant they maintained silence, coiled up like balls, cowering on their chairs. Then Therese, in a hollow voice, resumed:

"Did he seem to have suffered much?"

Laurent could not answer. He made a terrified gesture as if to put aside some hideous vision, and rising went towards the bed. Then, returning violently with open arms, he advanced towards Therese.

"Kiss me," said he, extending his neck.

Therese had risen, looking quite pale in her nightdress, and stood half thrown back, with her elbow resting on the marble mantelpiece. She gazed at the neck of her husband. On the white skin she had just caught sight of a pink spot. The rush of blood to the head, increased the size of this spot, turning it bright red.

"Kiss me, kiss me," repeated Laurent, his face and neck scarlet.

The young woman threw her head further back, to avoid an embrace, and pressing the tip of her finger on the bite Camille had given her husband, addressed him thus:

"What have you here? I never noticed this wound before."

It seemed to Laurent as if the finger of Therese was boring a hole in his throat. At the contact of this finger, he suddenly started backward, uttering a suppressed cry of pain.

"That," he stammered, "that—"

He hesitated, but he could not lie, and in spite of himself, he told the truth.

"That is the bite Camille gave me. You know, in the boat. It is nothing. It has healed. Kiss me, kiss me."

And the wretch craned his neck which was burning him. He wanted Therese to kiss the scar, convinced that the lips of this woman would appease the thousand pricks lacerating his flesh, and with raised chin he presented his extended neck for the embrace. Therese, who was almost lying back on the marble chimney-piece, gave a supreme gesture of disgust, and in a supplicating voice exclaimed:

"Oh! no, not on that part. There is blood."

She sank down on the low chair, trembling, with her forehead between her hands. Laurent remained where he stood for a moment, looking stupid. Then, all at once, with the clutch of a wild beast, he grasped the head of Therese in his two great hands, and by force brought her lips to the bite he had received from Camille on his neck. For an instant he kept, he crushed, this head of a woman against his skin. Therese had given way, uttering hollow groans. She was choking on the neck of Laurent. When she had freed herself from his hands, she violently wiped her mouth, and spat in the fire. She had not said a word.

Laurent, ashamed of his brutality, began walking slowly from the bed to the window. Suffering alone—the horrible burn—had made him exact a kiss from Therese, and when her frigid lips met the scorching scar, he felt the pain more acutely. This kiss obtained by violence had just crushed him. The shock had been so painful, that for nothing in the world would he have received another.

He cast his eyes upon the woman with whom he was to live, and who sat shuddering, doubled up before the fire, turning her back to him; and he repeated to himself that he no longer loved this woman, and that she no longer loved him.

For nearly an hour Therese maintained her dejected attitude, while Laurent silently walked backward and forward. Both inwardly acknowledged, with terror, that their passion was dead, that they had killed it in killing Camille. The embers on the hearth were gently dying out; a sheet of bright, clear fire shone above the ashes. Little by little, the heat of the room had become stifling; the flowers were fading, making the thick air sickly, with their heavy odour.

Laurent, all at once, had an hallucination. As he turned round, coming from the window to the bed, he saw Camille in a dark corner, between the chimney and wardrobe. The face of his victim looked greenish and distorted, just as he had seen it on the slab at the Morgue. He remained glued to the carpet, fainting, leaning against a piece of furniture for support. At a hollow rattle in his throat, Therese raised her head.

"There, there!" exclaimed Laurent in a terrified tone.

With extended arm, he pointed to the dark corner where he perceived the sinister face of Camille. Therese, infected by his terror, went and pressed against him.

"It is his portrait," she murmured in an undertone, as if the face of her late husband could hear her.

"His portrait?" repeated Laurent, whose hair stood on end.

"Yes, you know, the painting you did," she replied. "My aunt was to have removed it to her room. No doubt she forgot to take it down."

"Really; his portrait," said he.

The murderer had some difficulty in recognising the canvas. In his trouble he forgot that it was he who had drawn those clashing strokes, who had spread on those dirty tints that now terrified him. Terror made him see the picture as it was, vile, wretchedly put together, muddy, displaying the grimacing face of a corpse on a black ground. His own work astonished and crushed him by its atrocious ugliness; particularly the two eyes which seemed floating in soft, yellowish orbits, reminding him exactly of the decomposed eyes of the drowned man at the Morgue. For a moment, he remained breathless, thinking Therese was telling an untruth to allay his fears. Then he distinguished the frame, and little by little became calm.

"Go and take it down," said he in a very low tone to the young woman.

"Oh! no, I'm afraid," she answered with a shiver.

Laurent began to tremble again. At moments the frame of the picture disappeared, and he only saw the two white eyes giving him a long, steady look.

"I beg you to go and unhook it," said he, beseeching his companion.

"No, no," she replied.

"We will turn it face to the wall, and then it will not frighten us," he suggested.

"No," said she, "I cannot do it."

The murderer, cowardly and humble, thrust the young woman towards the canvas, hiding behind her, so as to escape the gaze of the drowned man. But she escaped, and he wanted to brazen the matter out. Approaching the picture, he raised his hand in search of the nail, but the portrait gave such a long, crushing, ignoble look, that Laurent after seeking to stare it out, found himself vanquished, and started back overpowered, murmuring as he did so:

"No, you are right, Therese, we cannot do it. Your aunt shall take it down to-morrow."

He resumed his walk up and down, with bowed head, feeling the portrait was staring at him, following him with its eyes. At times, he could not prevent himself casting a side glance at the canvas; and, then, in the depth of the darkness, he still perceived the dull, deadened eyes of the drowned man. The thought that Camille was there, in a corner, watching him, present on his wedding night, examining Therese and himself, ended by driving him mad with terror and despair.

One circumstance, which would have brought a smile to the lips of anyone else, made him completely lose his head. As he stood before the fire, he heard a sort of scratching sound. He turned pale, imagining it came from the portrait, that Camille was descending from his frame. Then he discovered that the noise was at the small door opening on the staircase, and he looked at Therese who also showed signs of fear.

"There is someone on the staircase," he murmured. "Who can be coming that way?"

The young woman gave no answer. Both were thinking of the drowned man, and their temples became moist with icy perspiration. They sought refuge together at the end of the room, expecting to see the door suddenly open, and the corpse of Camille fall on the floor. As the sound continued, but more sharply and irregularly, they thought their victim must be tearing away the wood with his nails to get in. For the space of nearly five minutes, they dared not stir. Finally, a mewing was heard, and Laurent advancing, recognised the tabby cat belonging to Madame Raquin, which had been accidentally shut up in the room, and was endeavouring to get out by clawing at the door.

Francois, frightened by Laurent, sprang upon a chair at a bound. With hair on end and stiffened paws, he looked his new master in the face, in a harsh and cruel manner. The young man did not like cats, and Francois almost terrified him. In this moment of excitement and alarm, he imagined the cat was about to fly in his face to avenge Camille. He fancied the beast must know everything, that there were thoughts in his strangely dilated round eyes. The fixed gaze of the animal caused Laurent to lower his lids. As he was about to give Francois a kick, Therese exclaimed:

"Don't hurt him."

This sentence produced a strange impression on Laurent, and an absurd idea got into his head.

"Camille has entered into this cat," thought he. "I shall have to kill the beast. It looks like a human being."

He refrained from giving the kick, being afraid of hearing Francois speak to him with the voice of Camille. Then he said to himself that this animal knew too much, and that he should have to throw it out of the window. But he had not the pluck to accomplish his design. Francois maintained a fighting attitude. With claws extended, and back curved in sullen irritation, he followed the least movement of his enemy with superb tranquillity. The metallic sparkle of his eyes troubled Laurent, who hastened to open the dining-room door, and the cat fled with a shrill mew.

Therese had again seated herself before the extinguished fire. Laurent resumed his walk from bed to window. It was thus that they awaited day-light. They did not think of going to bed; their hearts were thoroughly dead. They had but one, single desire: to leave the room they were in, and where they were choking. They experienced a real discomfort in being shut up together, and in breathing the same atmosphere. They would have liked someone to be there to interrupt their privacy, to drag them from the cruel embarrassment in which they found themselves, sitting one before the other without opening their lips, and unable to resuscitate their love. Their long silences tortured them, silence loaded with bitter and despairing complaints, with mute reproaches, which they distinctly heard in the tranquil air.

Day came at last, a dirty, whitish dawn, bringing penetrating cold with it. When the room had filled with dim light, Laurent, who was shivering, felt calmer. He looked the portrait of Camille straight in the face, and saw it as it was, commonplace and puerile. He took it down, and shrugging his shoulders, called himself a fool. Therese had risen from the low chair, and was tumbling the bed about for the purpose of deceiving her aunt, so as to make her believe they had passed a happy night.

"Look here," Laurent brutally remarked to her, "I hope we shall sleep well to-night! There must be an end to this sort of childishness."

Therese cast a deep, grave glance at him.

"You understand," he continued. "I did not marry for the purpose of passing sleepless nights. We are just like children. It was you who disturbed me with your ghostly airs. To-night you will try to be gay, and not frighten me."

He forced himself to laugh without knowing why he did so.

"I will try," gloomily answered the young woman.

Such was the wedding night of Therese and Laurent.

CHAPTER XXII

The following nights proved still more cruel. The murderers had wished to pass this part of the twenty-four hours together, so as to be able to defend themselves against the drowned man, and by a strange effect, since they had been doing so, they shuddered the more. They were exasperated, and their nerves so irritated, that they underwent atrocious attacks of suffering and terror, at the exchange of a simple word or look. At the slightest conversation between them, at the least talk, they had alone, they began raving, and were ready to draw blood.

The sort of remorse Laurent experienced was purely physical. His body, his irritated nerves and trembling frame alone were afraid of the drowned man. His conscience was for nothing in his terror. He did not feel the least regret at having killed Camille. When he was calm, when the spectre did not happen to be there, he would have committed the murder over again, had he thought his interests absolutely required it.

During the daytime he laughed at himself for his fright, making up his mind to be stronger, and he harshly rebuked Therese, whom he accused of troubling him. According to what he said, it was Therese who shuddered, it was Therese alone who brought on the frightful scenes, at night, in the bedroom. And, as soon as night came, as soon as he found himself shut in with his wife, icy perspiration pearled on his skin, and his frame shook with childish terror.

He thus underwent intermittent nervous attacks that returned nightly, and threw his senses into confusion while showing him the hideous green face of his victim. These attacks resembled the accesses of some frightful illness, a sort of hysteria of murder. The name of illness, of nervous affection, was really the only one to give to the terror that Laurent experienced. His face became convulsed, his limbs rigid, his nerves could be seen knotting beneath his skin. The body suffered horribly, while the spirit remained absent. The wretch felt no repentance. His passion for Therese had conveyed a frightful evil to him, and that was all.

Therese also found herself a prey to these heavy shocks. But, in her terror, she showed herself a woman: she felt vague remorse, unavowed regret. She, at times, had an inclination to cast herself on her knees and beseech the spectre of Camille to pardon her, while swearing to appease it by repentance. Maybe Laurent perceived these acts of cowardice on the part of Therese, for when they were agitated by the common terror, he laid the blame on her, and treated her with brutality.

On the first nights, they were unable to go to bed. They waited for daylight, seated before the fire, or pacing to and fro as on the evening of the wedding-day. The thought of lying down, side by side, on the bed, caused them a sort of terrifying repugnance. By tacit consent, they avoided kissing one another, and they did not even look at their couch, which Therese tumbled about in the morning.

When overcome with fatigue, they slept for an hour or two in the armchairs, to awaken with a start, under the influence of the sinister denouement of some nightmare. On awakening, with limbs stiff and tired, shivering all over with discomfort and cold, their faces marbled with livid blotches, they contemplated one another in bewilderment astonished to see themselves there. And they displayed strange bashfulness towards each other, ashamed at showing their disgust and terror.

But they struggled against sleep as much as they could. They seated themselves, one on each side of the chimney, and talked of a thousand trifles, being very careful not to let the conversation drop. There was a broad space between them in front of the fire. When they turned their heads, they imagined that Camille had drawn a chair there, and occupied this space, warming his feet in a lugubrious, bantering fashion. This vision, which they had seen on the evening of the wedding-day, returned each night.

And this corpse taking a mute, but jeering part, in their interviews, this horribly disfigured body ever remaining there, overwhelmed them with continued anxiety. Not daring to move, they half blinded themselves staring at the scorching flames, and, when unable to resist any longer, they cast a timid glance aside, their eyes irritated by the glowing coal, created the vision, and conveyed to it a reddish glow.

Laurent, in the end, refused to remain seated any longer, without avowing the cause of this whim to Therese. The latter understood that he must see Camille as she saw him; and, in her turn, she declared that the heat made her feel ill, and that she would be more comfortable a few steps away from the chimney. Pushing back her armchair to the foot of the bed, she remained there overcome, while her husband resumed his walk in the room. From time to time, he opened the window, allowing the icy air of the cold January night to fill the apartment, and this calmed his fever.

For a week, the newly-married couple passed the nights in this fashion, dozing and getting a little rest in the daytime, Therese behind the counter in the shop, Laurent in his office. At night they belonged to pain and fear. And the strangest part of the whole business was the attitude they maintained towards each other. They did not utter one word of love, but feigned to have forgotten the past; and seemed to accept, to tolerate one another like sick people, feeling secret pity for their mutual sufferings.

Both hoped to conceal their disgust and fear, and neither seemed to think of the peculiar nights they passed, which should have enlightened them as to the real state of their beings. When they sat up until morning, barely exchanging a word, turning pale at the least sound, they looked as if they thought all newly-married folk conducted themselves in the same way, during the first days of their marriage. This was the clumsy hypocrisy of two fools.

They were soon so overcome by weariness that they one night decided to lie on the bed. They did not undress, but threw themselves, as they were, on the quilt, fearing lest their bare skins should touch, for they fancied they would receive a painful shock at the least contact. Then, when they had slept thus, in an anxious sleep, for two nights, they risked removing their clothes, and slipping between the sheets. But they remained apart, and took all sorts of precautions so as not to come together.

Therese got into bed first, and lay down close to the wall. Laurent waited until she had made herself quite comfortable, and then ventured to stretch himself out at the opposite edge of the mattress, so that there was a broad space between them. It was there that the corpse of Camille lay.

When the two murderers were extended under the same sheet, and had closed their eyes, they fancied they felt the damp corpse of their victim, lying in the middle of the bed, and turning their flesh icy cold. It was like a vile obstacle separating them. They were seized with fever and delirium, and this obstacle, in their minds, became material. They touched the corpse, they saw it spread out, like a greenish and dissolved shred of something, and they inhaled the infectious odour of this lump of human putrefaction. All their senses were in a state of hallucination, conveying intolerable acuteness to their sensations.

The presence of this filthy bedfellow kept them motionless, silent, abstracted with anguish. Laurent, at times, thought of taking Therese violently in his arms; but he dared not move. He said to himself that he could not extend his hand, without getting it full of the soft flesh of Camille. Next he fancied that the drowned man came to sleep between them so as to prevent them clasping one another, and he ended by understanding that Camille was jealous.

Nevertheless, ever and anon, they sought to exchange a timid kiss, to see what would happen. The young man jeered at his wife, and ordered her to embrace him. But their lips were so cold that it seemed as if the dead man had got between their mouths. Both felt disgusted. Therese shuddered with horror, and Laurent who heard her teeth chattering, railed at her:

"Why are you trembling?" he exclaimed. "Are you afraid of Camille? Ah! the poor man is as dead as a doornail at this moment."

Both avoided saying what made them shudder. When an hallucination brought the countenance of the drowned man before Therese, she closed her eyes, keeping her terror to herself, not daring to speak to her husband of her vision, lest she should bring on a still more terrible crisis. And it was just the same with Laurent. When driven to extremities, he, in a fit of despair, accused Therese of being afraid of Camille. The name, uttered aloud, occasioned additional anguish. The murderer raved.

"Yes, yes," he stammered, addressing the young woman, "you are afraid of Camille. I can see that plain enough! You are a silly thing, you have no pluck at all. Look here! just go to sleep quietly. Do you think your husband will come and pull you out of bed by the heels, because I happen to be sleeping with you?"

This idea that the drowned man might come and pull them out of bed by the heels, made the hair of Laurent stand on end, and he continued with greater violence, while still in the utmost terror himself.

"I shall have to take you some night to the cemetery. We will open the coffin Camille is in, and you will see what he looks like! Then you will perhaps cease being afraid. Go on, he doesn't know we threw him in the water."

Therese with her head under the bedclothes, was uttering smothered groans.

"We threw him into the water, because he was in our way," resumed her husband. "And we'll throw him in again, will we not? Don't act like a child. Show a little strength. It's silly to trouble our happiness. You see, my dear, when we are dead and underground, we shall be neither less nor more happy, because we cast an idiot in the Seine, and we shall have freely enjoyed our love which will have been an advantage. Come, give me a kiss."

The young woman kissed him, but she was icy cold, and half crazy, while he shuddered as much as she did.

For a fortnight Laurent was asking himself how he could kill Camille again. He had flung him in the water; and yet he was not dead enough, because he came every night to sleep in the bed of Therese. While the murderers thought that having committed the crime, they could love one another in peace, their resuscitated victim arrived to make their touch like ice. Therese was not a widow. Laurent found that he was mated to a woman who already had a drowned man for husband.

CHAPTER XXIII

Little by little, Laurent became furiously mad, and resolved to drive Camille from his bed. He had first of all slept with his clothes on, then he had avoided touching Therese. In rage and despair, he wanted, at last, to take his wife in his arms, and crush the spectre of his victim rather than leave her to it. This was a superb revolt of brutality.

The hope that the kisses of Therese would cure him of his insomnia, had alone brought him into the room of the young woman. When he had found himself there, in the position of master, he had become a prey to such atrocious attacks, that it had not even occurred to him to attempt the cure. And he had remained overwhelmed for three weeks, without remembering that he had done everything to obtain Therese, and now that she was in his possession, he could not touch her without increased suffering.

His excessive anguish drew him from this state of dejection. In the first moment of stupor, amid the strange discouragement of the wedding-night, he had forgotten the reasons that had urged him to marry. But his repeated bad dreams had aroused in him a feeling of sullen irritation, which triumphed over his cowardice, and restored his memory. He remembered he had married in order to drive away nightmare, by pressing his wife closely to his breast. Then, one night, he abruptly took Therese in his arms, and, at the risk of passing over the corpse of the drowned man, drew her violently to him.

The young woman, who was also driven to extremes, would have cast herself into the fire had she thought that flames would have purified her flesh, and delivered her from her woe. She returned Laurent his advances, determined to be either consumed by the caresses of this man, or to find relief in them.

And they clasped one another in a hideous embrace. Pain and horror took the place of love. When their limbs touched, it was like falling on live coal. They uttered a cry, pressing still closer together, so as not to leave room for the drowned man. But they still felt the shreds of Camille, which were ignobly squeezed between them, freezing their skins in parts, whilst in others they were burning hot.

Their kisses were frightfully cruel. Therese sought the bite that Camille had given in the stiff, swollen neck of Laurent, and passionately pressed her lips to it. There was the raw sore; this wound once healed, and the murderers would sleep in peace. The young woman understood this, and she endeavoured to cauterise the bad place with the fire of her caresses. But she scorched her lips, and Laurent thrust her violently away, giving a dismal groan. It seemed to him that she was pressing a red-hot iron to his neck. Therese, half mad, came back. She wanted to kiss the scar again. She experienced a keenly voluptuous sensation in placing her mouth on this piece of skin wherein Camille had buried his teeth.

At one moment she thought of biting her husband in the same place, of tearing away a large piece of flesh, of making a fresh and deeper wound, that would remove the trace of the old one. And she said to herself that she would no more turn pale when she saw the marks of her own teeth. But Laurent shielded his neck from her kisses. The smarting pain he experienced was too acute, and each time his wife presented her lips, he pushed her back. They struggled in this manner with a rattling in their throats, writhing in the horror of their caresses.

They distinctly felt that they only increased their suffering. They might well strain one another in these terrible clasps, they cried out with pain, they burnt and bruised each other, but were unable to calm their frightfully excited nerves. Each strain rendered their disgust more intense. While exchanging these ghastly embraces, they were a prey to the most terrible hallucinations, imagining that the drowned man was dragging them by the heels, and violently jerking the bedstead.

For a moment they let one another go, feeling repugnance and invincible nervous agitation. Then they determined not to be conquered. They clasped each other again in a fresh embrace, and once more were obliged to separate, for it seemed as if red-hot bradawls were entering their limbs. At several intervals they attempted in this way to overcome their disgust, by tiring, by wearing out their nerves. And each time their nerves became irritated and strained, causing them such exasperation, that they would perhaps have died of enervation had they remained in the arms of one another. This battle against their own bodies excited them to madness, and they obstinately sought to gain the victory. Finally, a more acute crisis exhausted them. They received a shock of such incredible violence that they thought they were about to have a fit.

Cast back one on each side of the bed, burning and bruised, they began to sob. And amidst their tears, they seemed to hear the triumphant laughter of the drowned man, who again slid, chuckling, under the sheet. They had been unable to drive him from the bed and were vanquished. Camille gently stretched himself between them, whilst Laurent deplored his want of power to thrust him away, and Therese trembled lest the corpse should have the idea of taking advantage of the victory to press her, in his turn, in his arms, in the quality of legitimate master.

They had made a supreme effort. In face of their defeat, they understood that, in future, they dared not exchange the smallest kiss. What they had attempted, in order to drive away their terror, had plunged them into greater fright. And, as they felt the chill of the corpse, which was now to separate them for ever, they shed bitter tears, asking themselves, with anguish, what would become of them.

CHAPTER XXIV

In accordance with the hopes of old Michaud, when doing his best to bring about the marriage of Therese and Laurent, the Thursday evenings resumed their former gaiety, as soon as the wedding was over.

These evenings were in great peril at the time of the death of Camille. The guests came, in fear, into this house of mourning; each week they were trembling with anxiety, lest they should be definitely dismissed.

The idea that the door of the shop would no doubt at last be closed to them, terrified Michaud and Grivet, who clung to their habits with the instinct and obstinacy of brutes. They said to themselves that the old woman and young widow would one day go and weep over the defunct at Vernon or elsewhere, and then, on Thursday nights, they would not know what to do. In the mind's eye they saw themselves wandering about the arcade in a lamentable fashion, dreaming of colossal games at dominoes.

Pending the advent of these bad times, they timidly enjoyed their final moments of happiness, arriving with an anxious, sugary air at the shop, and repeating to themselves, on each occasion, that they would perhaps return no more. For over a year they were beset with these fears. In face of the tears of Madame Raquin and the silence of Therese, they dared not make themselves at ease and laugh. They felt they were no longer at home as in the time of Camille; it seemed, so to say, that they were stealing every evening they passed seated at the dining-room table. It was in these desperate circumstances that the egotism of Michaud urged him to strike a masterly stroke by finding a husband for the widow of the drowned man.

On the Thursday following the marriage, Grivet and Michaud made a triumphant entry into the dining-room. They had conquered. The dining-room belonged to them again. They no longer feared dismissal. They came there as happy people, stretching out their legs, and cracking their former jokes, one after the other. It could be seen from their delighted and confident attitude that, in their idea, a revolution had been accomplished. All recollection of Camille had been dispelled. The dead husband, the spectre that cast a chill over everyone, had been driven away by the living husband. The past and its joys were resuscitated. Laurent took the place of Camille, all cause for sadness disappeared, the guests could now laugh without grieving anyone; and, indeed, it was their duty to laugh to cheer up this worthy family who were good enough to receive them.

Henceforth, Grivet and Michaud, who for nearly eighteen months had visited the house under the pretext of consoling Madame Raquin, could set their little hypocrisy aside, and frankly come and doze opposite one another to the sharp ring of the dominoes.

And each week brought a Thursday evening, each week those lifeless and grotesque heads which formerly had exasperated Therese, assembled round the table. The young woman talked of showing these folk the door; their bursts of foolish laughter and silly reflections irritated her. But Laurent made her understand that such a step would be a mistake; it was necessary that the present should resemble the past as much as possible; and, above all, they must preserve the friendship of the police, of those idiots who protected them from all suspicion. Therese gave way. The guests were well received, and they viewed with delight a future full of a long string of warm Thursday evenings.

It was about this time that the lives of the couple became, in a way, divided in two.

In the morning, when day drove away the terror of night, Laurent hastily dressed himself. But he only recovered his ease and egotistic calm when in the dining-room, seated before an enormous bowl of coffee and milk, which Therese prepared for him. Madame Raquin, who had become even more feeble and could barely get down to the shop, watched him eating with a maternal smile. He swallowed the toast, filled his stomach and little by little became tranquillised. After the coffee, he drank a small glass of brandy which completely restored him. Then he said "good-bye" to Madame Raquin and Therese, without ever kissing them, and strolled to his office.

Spring was at hand; the trees along the quays were becoming covered with leaves, with light, pale green lacework. The river ran with caressing sounds below; above, the first sunny rays of the year shed gentle warmth. Laurent felt himself another man in the fresh air; he freely inhaled this breath of young life descending from the skies of April and May; he sought the sun, halting to watch the silvery reflection streaking the Seine, listening to the sounds on the quays, allowing the acrid odours of early day to penetrate him, enjoying the clear, delightful morn.

He certainly thought very little about Camille. Sometimes he listlessly contemplated the Morgue on the other side of the water, and his mind then reverted to his victim, like a man of courage might think of a silly fright that had come over him. With stomach full, and face refreshed, he recovered his thick-headed tranquillity. He reached his office, and passed the whole day gaping, and awaiting the time to leave. He was a mere clerk like the others, stupid and weary, without an idea in his head, save that of sending in his resignation and taking a studio. He dreamed vaguely of a new existence of idleness, and this sufficed to occupy him until evening.

Thoughts of the shop in the arcade never troubled him. At night, after longing for the hour of release since the morning, he left his office with regret, and followed the quays again, secretly troubled and anxious. However slowly he walked, he had to enter the shop at last, and there terror awaited him.

Therese experienced the same sensations. So long as Laurent was not beside her, she felt at ease. She had dismissed her charwoman, saying that everything was in disorder, and the shop and apartment filthy dirty. She all at once had ideas of tidiness. The truth was that she felt the necessity of moving about, of doing something, of exercising her stiff limbs. She went hither and thither all the morning, sweeping, dusting, cleaning the rooms, washing up the plates and dishes, doing work that would have disgusted her formerly. These household duties kept her on her feet, active and silent, until noon, without allowing her time to think of aught else than the cobwebs hanging from the ceiling and the greasy plates.

On the stroke of twelve, she went to the kitchen to prepare lunch. At table, Madame Raquin was pained to see her always rising to fetch the dishes; she was touched and annoyed at the activity displayed by her niece; she scolded her, and Therese replied that it was necessary to economise. When the meal was over, the young woman dressed, and at last decided to join her aunt behind the counter. There, sleep overtook her; worn out by her restless nights, she dozed off, yielding to the voluptuous feeling of drowsiness that gained her, as soon as she sat down.

These were only light spells of heaviness, replete with vague charm that calmed her nerves. The thoughts of Camille left her; she enjoyed that tranquil repose of invalids who are all at once freed from pain. She felt relieved in body, her mind free, she sank into a gentle and repairing state of nothingness. Deprived of these few calm moments, she would have broken down under the tension of her nervous system. These spells of somnolence gave her strength to suffer again, and become terrified the ensuing night. As a matter of fact she did not sleep, she barely closed her lids, and was lost in a dream of peace. When a customer entered, she opened her eyes, served the few sous worth of articles asked for, and fell back into the floating reverie.

In this manner she passed three or four hours of perfect happiness, answering her aunt in monosyllables, and yielding with real enjoyment to these moments of unconsciousness which relieved her of her thoughts, and completely overcame her. She barely, at long intervals, cast a glance into the arcade, and was particularly at her ease in cloudy weather, when it was dark and she could conceal her lassitude in the gloom.

The damp and disgusting arcade, crossed by a lot of wretched drenched pedestrians, whose umbrellas dripped upon the tiles, seemed to her like an alley in a low quarter, a sort of dirty, sinister corridor, where no one would come to seek and trouble her. At moments, when she saw the dull gleams of light that hung around her, when she smelt the bitter odour of the dampness, she imagined she had just been buried alive, that she was underground, at the bottom of a common grave swarming with dead. And this thought consoled and appeased her, for she said to herself that she was now in security, that she was about to die and would suffer no more.

But sometimes she had to keep her eyes open; Suzanne paid her a visit, and remained embroidering near the counter all the afternoon. The wife of Olivier, with her putty face and slow movements, now pleased Therese, who experienced strange relief in observing this poor, broken-up creature, and had made a friend of her. She loved to see her at her side, smiling with her faint smile, more dead than alive, and bringing into the shop the stuffy odour of the cemetery. When the blue eyes of Suzanne, transparent as glass, rested fixedly on those of Therese, the latter experienced a beneficent chill in the marrow of her bones.

Therese remained thus until four o'clock, when she returned to the kitchen, and there again sought fatigue, preparing dinner for Laurent with febrile haste. But when her husband appeared on the threshold she felt a tightening in the throat, and all her being once more became a prey to anguish.

Each day, the sensations of the couple were practically the same. During the daytime, when they were not face to face, they enjoyed delightful hours of repose; at night, as soon as they came together, both experienced poignant discomfort.

The evenings, nevertheless, were calm. Therese and Laurent, who shuddered at the thought of going to their room, sat up as long as possible. Madame Raquin, reclining in a great armchair, was placed between them, and chatted in her placid voice. She spoke of Vernon, still thinking of her son, but avoiding to mention him from a sort of feeling of diffidence for the others; she smiled at her dear children, and formed plans for their future. The lamp shed its faint gleams on her white face, and her words sounded particularly sweet in the silence and stillness of the room.

The murderers, one seated on each side of her, silent and motionless, seemed to be attentively listening to what she said. In truth they did not attempt to follow the sense of the gossip of the good old lady. They were simply pleased to hear this sound of soft words which prevented them attending the crash of their own thoughts. They dared not cast their eyes on one another, but looked at Madame Raquin to give themselves countenances. They never breathed a word about going to bed; they would have remained there until morning, listening to the affectionate nonsense of the former mercer, amid the appeasement she spread around her, had she not herself expressed the desire to retire. It was only then that they quitted the dining-room and entered their own apartment in despair, as if casting themselves to the bottom of an abyss.

But they soon had much more preference for the Thursday gatherings, than for these family evenings. When alone with Madame Raquin, they were unable to divert their thoughts; the feeble voice of their aunt, and her tender gaiety, did not stifle the cries that lacerated them. They could feel bedtime coming on, and they shuddered when their eyes caught sight of the door of their room. Awaiting the moment when they would be alone, became more and more cruel as the evening advanced. On Thursday night, on the contrary, they were giddy with folly, one forgot the presence of the other, and they suffered less. Therese ended by heartily longing for the reception days. Had Michaud and Grivet not arrived, she would have gone and fetched them. When strangers were in the dining-room, between herself and Laurent, she felt more calm. She would have liked to always have guests there, to hear a noise, something to divert her, and detach her from her thoughts. In the presence of other people, she displayed a sort of nervous gaiety. Laurent also recovered his previous merriment, returning to his coarse peasant jests, his hoarse laughter, his practical jokes of a former canvas dauber. Never had these gatherings been so gay and noisy.

It was thus that Laurent and Therese could remain face to face, once a week, without shuddering.

But they were soon beset with further anxiety. Paralysis was little by little gaining on Madame Raquin, and they foresaw the day when she would be riveted to her armchair, feeble and doltish. The poor old lady already began to stammer fragments of disjointed phrases; her voice was growing weaker, and her limbs were one by one losing their vitality. She was becoming a thing. It was with terror that Therese and Laurent observed the breaking up of this being who still separated them, and whose voice drew them from their bad dreams. When the old mercer lost her intelligence, and remained stiff and silent in her armchair, they would find themselves alone, and in the evening would no longer be able to escape the dreadful face to face conversation. Then their terror would commence at six o'clock instead of midnight. It would drive them mad.

They made every effort to give Madame Raquin that health which had become so necessary to them. They called in doctors, and bestowed on the patient all sorts of little attentions. Even this occupation of nurses caused them to forget, and afforded them an appeasement that encouraged them to double in zeal. They did not wish to lose a third party who rendered their evenings supportable; and they did not wish the dining-room and the whole house to become a cruel and sinister spot like their room.

Madame Raquin was singularly touched at the assiduous care they took of her. She applauded herself, amid tears, at having united them, and at having abandoned to them her forty thousand francs. Never, since the death of her son, had she counted on so much affection in her final moments. Her old age was quite softened by the tenderness of her dear children. She did not feel the implacable paralysis which, in spite of all, made her more and more rigid day by day.

Nevertheless, Therese and Laurent continued to lead their double existence. In each of them there were like two distinct beings: a nervous, terrified being who shuddered as soon as dusk set in, and a torpid forgetful being, who breathed at ease when the sun rose. They lived two lives, crying out in anguish when alone, and peacefully smiling in company. Never did their faces, in public, show the slightest trace of the sufferings that had reached them in private. They appeared calm and happy, and instinctively concealed their troubles.

To see them so tranquil in the daytime, no one would have suspected the hallucinations that tortured them every night. They would have been taken for a couple blessed by heaven, and living in the enjoyment of full felicity. Grivet gallantly called them the "turtle-doves." When he jested about their fatigued looks, Laurent and Therese barely turned pale, and even succeeded in forcing on a smile. They became accustomed to the naughty jokes of the old clerk.

So long as they remained in the dining-room, they were able to keep their terror under control. The mind could not imagine the frightful change that came over them, as soon as they were shut up in their bedroom. On the Thursday night, particularly, this transformation was so violently brutal, that it seemed as if accomplished in a supernatural world. The drama in the bedroom, by its strangeness, by its savage passion, surpassed all belief, and remained deeply concealed within their aching beings. Had they spoken of it, they would have been taken for mad.

"How happy those sweethearts are!" frequently remarked old Michaud. "They hardly say a word, but that does not prevent them thinking. I bet they devour one another with kisses when we have gone."

Such was the opinion of the company. Therese and Laurent came to be spoken of as a model couple. All the tenants in the Arcade of the Pont Neuf extolled the affection, the tranquil happiness, the everlasting honeymoon of the married pair. They alone knew that the corpse of Camille slept between them; they alone felt, beneath the calm exterior of their faces, the nervous contractions that, at night, horribly distorted their features, and changed the placid expression of their physiognomies into hideous masks of pain.

CHAPTER XXV

At the expiration of four months, Laurent thought of taking advantage of the profit he had calculated on deriving from his marriage. He would have abandoned his wife, and fled from the spectre of Camille, three days after the wedding, had not his interest detained him at the shop in the arcade. He accepted his nights of terror, he remained in the anguish that was choking him, so as not to be deprived of the benefit of his crime.

If he parted from Therese, he would again be plunged in poverty, and be forced to retain his post; by remaining with her, he would, on the contrary, be able to satisfy his inclination for idleness, and to live liberally, doing nothing, on the revenue Madame Raquin had placed in the name of his wife. Very likely he would have fled with the 40,000 francs, had he been able to realise them; but the old mercer, on the advice of Michaud, had shown the prudence to protect the interests of her niece in the marriage contract.

Laurent, in this manner, found himself attached to Therese by a powerful bond. As a set-off against his atrocious nights, he determined at least to be kept in blissful laziness, well fed, warmly clothed, and provided with the necessary cash in his pocket to satisfy his whims. At this price alone, would he consent to sleep with the corpse of the drowned man.

One evening, he announced to Madame Raquin and his wife that he had sent in his resignation, and would quit his office at the end of a fortnight. Therese gave a gesture of anxiety. He hastened to add that he intended taking a small studio where he would go on with his painting. He spoke at length about the annoyance of his employment, and the broad horizons that Art opened to him. Now that he had a few sous and could make a bid for success, he wished to see whether he was not capable of great achievements.

The speech he made on this subject simply concealed a ferocious desire to resume his former studio life. Therese sat with pinched lips without replying; she had no idea of allowing Laurent to squander the small fortune that assured her liberty. When her husband pressed her with questions in view of obtaining her consent, she answered curtly, giving him to understand that if he left his office, he would no longer be earning any money, and would be living entirely at her expense.

But, as she spoke, Laurent observed her so keenly, that he troubled her, and arrested on her lips the refusal she was about to utter. She fancied she read in the eyes of her accomplice, this menacing threat:

"If you do not consent, I shall reveal everything."

She began to stammer, and Madame Raquin exclaimed that the desire of her dear son was no more than what was just, and that they must give him the means to become a man of talent. The good lady spoilt Laurent as she had spoilt Camille. Quite mollified by the caresses the young man lavished on her, she belonged to him, and never failed to take his part.

It was therefore decided that Laurent should have a studio, and receive one hundred francs a month pocket-money. The budget of the family was arranged in this way: the profits realised in the mercery business would pay the rent of the shop and apartment, and the balance would almost suffice for the daily expenses of the family; Laurent would receive the rent of his studio and his one hundred francs a month, out of the two thousand and a few hundred francs income from the funded money, the remainder going into the general purse. In that way the capital would remain intact. This arrangement somewhat tranquillised Therese, who nevertheless made her husband swear that he would never go beyond the sum allowed him. But as to that matter, she said to herself that Laurent could not get possession of the 40,000 francs without her signature, and she was thoroughly determined that she would never place her name to any document.

On the morrow, Laurent took a small studio in the lower part of the Rue Mazarine, which his eye had been fixed on for a month. He did not mean to leave his office without having a refuge where he could quietly pass his days far away from Therese. At the end of the fortnight, he bade adieu to his colleagues. Grivet was stupefied at his departure. A young man, said he, who had such a brilliant future before him, a young man who in the space of four years, had reached a salary that he, Grivet, had taken twenty years to attain! Laurent stupefied him still more, when he told him he was going to give his whole time to painting.

At last the artist installed himself in his studio, which was a sort of square loft about seven or eight yards long by the same breadth. The ceiling which inclined abruptly in a rapid slope, was pierced by a large window conveying a white raw light to the floor and blackish walls. The sounds in the street did not ascend so high. This silent, wan room, opening above on the sky, resembled a hole, or a vault dug out of grey clay. Laurent furnished the place anywise; he brought a couple of chairs with holes in the rush seats, a table that he set against the wall so that it might not slip down, an old kitchen dresser, his colour-box and easel; all the luxury in the place consisted of a spacious divan which he purchased for thirty francs from a second-hand dealer.

He remained a fortnight without even thinking of touching his brushes. He arrived between eight and nine o'clock in the morning, smoked, stretched himself on the divan, and awaited noon, delighted that it was morning, and that he had many hours of daylight before him. At twelve he went to lunch. As soon as the meal was over, he hastened back, to be alone, and get away from the pale face of Therese. He next went through the process of digestion, sleeping spread out on the divan until evening. His studio was an abode of peace where he did not tremble. One day his wife asked him if she might visit this dear refuge. He refused, and as, notwithstanding his refusal, she came and knocked at the door, he refrained from opening to her, telling her in the evening that he had spent the day at the Louvre Museum. He was afraid that Therese might bring the spectre of Camille with her.

Idleness ended by weighing heavily on his shoulders, so he purchased a canvas and colours, and set to work. As he had not sufficient money to pay models, he resolved to paint according to fancy, without troubling about nature, and he began the head of a man.

But at this time, he did not shut himself up so much as he had done; he worked for two or three hours every morning and passed the afternoon strolling hither and thither in Paris and its vicinity. It was opposite the Institut, on his return from one of these long walks, that he knocked up against his old college friend, who had met with a nice little success, thanks to the good fellowship of his comrades, at the last Salon.

"What, is it you?" exclaimed the painter. "Ah! my poor Laurent, I hardly recognise you. You have lost flesh."

"I am married," answered Laurent in an embarrassed tone.

"Married, you!" said the other. "Then I am not surprised to see you look so funny: and what are you doing now?"

"I have taken a small studio," replied Laurent; "and I paint a little, in the morning."

Then, in a feverish voice, he briefly related the story of his marriage, and explained his future plans. His friend observed him with an air of astonishment that troubled and alarmed him. The truth was that the painter no longer found in the husband of Therese, the coarse, common fellow he had known formerly. It seemed to him that Laurent was acquiring a gentlemanly bearing; his face had grown thinner, and had taken the pale tint of good taste, while his whole frame looked more upright and supple.

"But you are becoming a handsome chap," the artist could not refrain from exclaiming. "You are dressed like an ambassador, in the latest style. Who's your model?"

Laurent, who felt the weight of the examination he was undergoing, did not dare to abruptly take himself off.

"Will you come up to my studio for a moment?" he at last asked his friend, who showed no signs of leaving him.

"Willingly," answered the latter.

The painter, who could not understand the change he noticed in his old comrade, was anxious to visit his studio. He had no idea of climbing five floors to gaze on the new pictures of Laurent, which assuredly would disgust him; he merely wished to satisfy his curiosity.

When he had reached the studio, and had glanced at the canvases hanging against the walls, his astonishment redoubled. They comprised five studies, two heads of women, and three of men painted with real vigour. They looked thick and substantial, each part being dashed off with magnificent dabs of colour on a clear grey background. The artist quickly approached, and was so astounded that he did not even seek to conceal his amazement.

"Did you do those?" he inquired of Laurent.

"Yes," replied the latter. "They are studies that I intend to utilise in a large picture I am preparing."

"Come, no humbug, are you really the author of those things?"

"Eh! Yes. Why should I not be the author of them?"

The painter did not like to answer what he thought, which was as follows:

"Because those canvases are the work of an artist, and you have never been anything but a vile bungler."

For a long time, he remained before the studies in silence. Certainly they were clumsy, but they were original, and so powerfully executed

Emile Zola

that they indicated a highly developed idea of art. They were life-like. Never had this friend of Laurent seen rough painting so full of high promise. When he had examined all the canvases, he turned to the author of them and said:

"Well, frankly, I should never have thought you capable of painting like that. Where the deuce did you learn to have talent? It is not usually a thing that one acquires."

And he considered Laurent, whose voice appeared to him more gentle, while every gesture he made had a sort of elegance. The artist had no idea of the frightful shock this man had received, and which had transformed him, developing in him the nerves of a woman, along with keen, delicate sensations. No doubt a strange phenomenon had been accomplished in the organism of the murderer of Camille. It is difficult for analysis to penetrate to such depths. Laurent had, perhaps, become an artist as he had become afraid, after the great disorder that had upset his frame and mind.

Previously, he had been half choked by the fulness of his blood, blinded by the thick vapour of breath surrounding him. At present, grown thin, and always shuddering, his manner had become anxious, while he experienced the lively and poignant sensations of a man of nervous temperament. In the life of terror that he led, his mind had grown delirious, ascending to the ecstasy of genius. The sort of moral malady, the neurosis wherewith all his being was agitated, had developed an artistic feeling of peculiar lucidity. Since he had killed, his frame seemed lightened, his distracted mind appeared to him immense; and, in this abrupt expansion of his thoughts, he perceived exquisite creations, the reveries of a poet passing before his eyes. It was thus that his gestures had suddenly become elegant, that his works were beautiful, and were all at once rendered true to nature, and life-like.

The friend did not seek further to fathom the mystery attending this birth of the artist. He went off carrying his astonishment along with him. But before he left, he again gazed at the canvases and said to Laurent:

"I have only one thing to reproach you with: all these studies have a family likeness. The five heads resemble each other. The women, themselves, have a peculiarly violent bearing that gives them the appearance of men in disguise. You will understand that if you desire to make a picture out of these studies, you must change some of the phys-

147

iognomies; your personages cannot all be brothers, or brothers and sisters, it would excite hilarity."

He left the studio, and on the landing merrily added:

"Really, my dear boy, I am very pleased to have seen you. Henceforth, I shall believe in miracles. Good heavens! How highly respectable you do look!"

As he went downstairs, Laurent returned to the studio, feeling very much upset. When his friend had remarked that all his studies of heads bore a family likeness, he had abruptly turned round to conceal his paleness. The fact was that he had already been struck by this fatal resemblance. Slowly entering the room, he placed himself before the pictures, and as he contemplated them, as he passed from one to the other, icelike perspiration moistened his back.

"He is quite right," he murmured, "they all resemble one another. They resemble Camille."

He retired a step or two, and seated himself on the divan, unable to remove his eyes from the studies of heads. The first was an old man with a long white beard; and under this white beard, the artist traced the lean chin of Camille. The second represented a fair young girl, who gazed at him with the blue eyes of his victim. Each of the other three faces presented a feature of the drowned man. It looked like Camille with the theatrical make-up of an old man, of a young girl, assuming whatever disguise it pleased the painter to give him, but still maintaining the general expression of his own countenance.

There existed another terrible resemblance among these heads: they all appeared suffering and terrified, and seemed as though overburdened with the same feeling of horror. Each of them had a slight wrinkle to the left of the mouth, which drawing down the lips, produced a grimace. This wrinkle, which Laurent remembered having noticed on the convulsed face of the drowned man, marked them all with a sign of vile relationship.

Laurent understood that he had taken too long a look at Camille at the Morgue. The image of the drowned man had become deeply impressed on his mind; and now, his hand, without his being conscious of it, never failed to draw the lines of this atrocious face which followed him everywhere.

Little by little, the painter, who was allowing himself to fall back on the divan, fancied he saw the faces become animated. He had five

Camilles before him, five Camilles whom his own fingers had power-fully created, and who, by terrifying peculiarity were of various ages and of both sexes. He rose, he lacerated the pictures and threw them outside. He said to himself that he would die of terror in his studio, were he to people it with portraits of his victim.

A fear had just come over him: he dreaded that he would no more be able to draw a head without reproducing that of the drowned man. He wished to ascertain, at once, whether he were master of his own hand. He placed a white canvas on his easel; and, then, with a bit of charcoal, sketched out a face in a few lines. The face resembled Camille. Laurent swiftly effaced this drawing and tried another.

For an hour he struggled against futility, which drove along his fingers. At each fresh attempt, he went back to the head of the drowned man. He might indeed assert his will, and avoid the lines he knew so well. In spite of himself, he drew those lines, he obeyed his muscles and his rebellious nerves. He had first of all proceeded rapidly with his sketches; he now took pains to pass the stick of charcoal slowly over the canvas. The result was the same: Camille, grimacing and in pain, appeared ceaselessly.

The artist sketched the most different heads successively: the heads of angels, of virgins with aureoles, of Roman warriors with their helmets, of fair, rosy children, of old bandits seamed with scars; and the drowned man always, always reappeared; he became, in turn, angel, virgin, warrior, child and bandit.

Then, Laurent plunged into caricature: he exaggerated the features, he produced monstrous profiles, he invented grotesque heads, but only succeeded in rendering the striking portrait of his victim more horrible. He finished by drawing animals, dogs and cats; but even the dogs and cats vaguely resembled Camille.

Laurent then became seized with sullen rage. He smashed the canvas with his fist, thinking in despair of his great picture. Now, he must put that idea aside; he was convinced that, in future, he would draw nothing but the head of Camille, and as his friend had told him, faces all alike would cause hilarity. He pictured to himself what his work would have been, and perceived upon the shoulders of his personages, men and women, the livid and terrified face of the drowned man. The strange picture he thus conjured up, appeared to him atrociously ridiculous and exasperated him.

He no longer dared to paint, always dreading that he would resuscitate his victim at the least stroke of his brush. If he desired to live peacefully in his studio he must never paint there. This thought that his fingers possessed the fatal and unconscious faculty of reproducing without end the portrait of Camille, made him observe his hand in terror. It seemed to him that his hand no longer belonged to him.

CHAPTER XXVI

The crisis threatening Madame Raquin took place. The paralysis, which for several months had been creeping along her limbs, always ready to strangle her, at last took her by the throat and linked her body. One evening, while conversing peacefully with Therese and Laurent, she remained in the middle of a sentence with her mouth wide open: she felt as if she was being throttled. When she wanted to cry out and call for help, she could only splutter a few hoarse sounds. Her hands and feet were rigid. She found herself struck dumb, and powerless to move.

Therese and Laurent rose from their chairs, terrified at this stroke, which had contorted the old mercer in less than five seconds. When she became rigid, and fixed her supplicating eyes on them, they pressed her with questions in order to ascertain the cause of her suffering. Unable to reply, she continued gazing at them in profound anguish.

They then understood that they had nothing but a corpse before them, a corpse half alive that could see and hear, but could not speak to them. They were in despair at this attack. At the bottom of their hearts, they cared little for the suffering of the paralysed woman. They mourned over themselves, who in future would have to live alone, face to face.

From this day the life of the married couple became intolerable. They passed the most cruel evenings opposite the impotent old lady, who no longer lulled their terror with her gentle, idle chatter. She reposed in an armchair, like a parcel, a thing, while they remained alone, one at each end of the table, embarrassed and anxious. This body no longer separated them; at times they forgot it, confounding it with the articles of furniture.

They were now seized with the same terror as at night. The dining-room became, like the bedroom, a terrible spot, where the spectre of Camille arose, causing them to suffer an extra four or five hours daily. As soon as twilight came, they shuddered, lowering the lamp-shade so as not to see one another, and endeavouring to persuade themselves that Madame Raquin was about to speak and thus remind them of her presence. If they kept her with them, if they did not get rid of her, it was because her eyes were still alive, and they experienced a little relief in watching them move and sparkle.

They always placed the impotent old lady in the bright beam of the lamp, so as to thoroughly light up her face and have it always before them. This flabby, livid countenance would have been a sight that others could not have borne, but Therese and Laurent experienced such need for company, that they gazed upon it with real joy.

This face looked like that of a dead person in the centre of which two living eyes had been fixed. These eyes alone moved, rolling rapidly in their orbits. The cheeks and mouth maintained such appalling immobility that they seemed as though petrified. When Madame Raquin fell asleep and lowered her lids, her countenance, which was then quite white and mute, was really that of a corpse. Therese and Laurent, who no longer felt anyone with them, then made a noise until the paralysed woman raised her eyelids and looked at them. In this manner they compelled her to remain awake.

They regarded her as a distraction that drew them from their bad dreams. Since she had been infirm, they had to attend to her like a child. The care they lavished on her forced them to scatter their thoughts. In the morning Laurent lifted her up and bore her to her armchair; at night he placed her on her bed again. She was still heavy, and he had to exert all his strength to raise her delicately in his arms, and carry her. It was also he who rolled her armchair along. The other attentions fell to Therese. She dressed and fed the impotent old lady, and sought to understand her slightest wish.

For a few days Madame Raquin preserved the use of her hands. She could write on a slate, and in this way asked for what she required; then the hands withered, and it became impossible for her to raise them or hold a pencil. From that moment her eyes were her only language, and it was necessary for her niece to guess what she desired. The young woman devoted herself to the hard duties of sick-nurse, which gave her occupation for body and mind that did her much good.

So as not to remain face to face, the married couple rolled the armchair of the poor old lady into the dining-room, the first thing in the morning. They placed her between them, as if she were necessary to their existence. They caused her to be present at their meals, and at all their interviews. When she signified the desire to retire to her bedroom, they feigned not to understand. She was only of use to interrupt their private conversations, and had no right to live apart.

At eight o'clock, Laurent went to his studio, Therese descended to the shop, while the paralyzed woman remained alone in the dining-room until noon; then, after lunch, she found herself without company again until six o'clock. Frequently, during the day, her niece ran upstairs, and, hovering round her, made sure she did not require anything. The friends of the family were at a loss for sufficiently laudatory phrases wherein to extol the virtues of Therese and Laurent.

The Thursday receptions continued, the impotent old lady being present, as in the past. Her armchair was advanced to the table, and from eight o'clock till eleven she kept her eyes open, casting penetrating glances from one to another of her guests in turn. On the first few of these evenings, old Michaud and Grivet felt some embarrassment in the presence of the corpse of their old friend. They did not know what countenance to put on. They only experienced moderate sorrow, and they were inquiring in their minds in what measure it would be suitable to display their grief. Should they speak to this lifeless form? Should they refrain from troubling about it? Little by little, they decided to treat Madame Raquin as though nothing had happened to her. They ended by feigning to completely ignore her condition. They chatted with her, putting questions and giving the answers, laughing both for her and for themselves, and never permitting the rigid expression on the countenance to baffle them.

It was a strange sight: these men who appeared to be speaking sensibly to a statue, just as little girls talk to their dolls. The paralysed woman sat rigid and mute before them, while they babbled, multiplying their gestures in exceedingly animated conversations with her. Michaud and Grivet prided themselves on their correct attitude. In acting as they did, they believed they were giving proof of politeness; they, moreover, avoided the annoyance of the customary condolences. They fancied that Madame Raquin must feel flattered to find herself treated as a person in good health; and, from that moment, it became possible for them to be merry in her presence, without the least scruple.

Grivet had contracted a mania. He affirmed that Madame Raquin and himself understood one another perfectly; and that she could not look at him without him at once comprehending what she desired. This was another delicate attention. Only Grivet was on every occasion in error. He frequently interrupted the game of dominoes, to observe the infirm woman whose eyes were quietly following the game, and declare that she wanted such or such a thing. On further inquiry it was found that she wanted nothing at all, or that she wanted something entirely different. This did not discourage Grivet, who triumphantly exclaimed:

"Just as I said!" And he began again a few moments later.

It was quite another matter when the impotent old lady openly expressed a desire; Therese, Laurent, and the guests named one object after another that they fancied she might wish for. Grivet then made himself remarkable by the clumsiness of his offers. He mentioned, haphazard, everything that came into his head, invariably offering the contrary to what Madame Raquin desired. But this circumstance did not prevent him repeating:

"I can read in her eyes as in a book. Look, she says I am right. Is it not so, dear lady? Yes, yes."

Nevertheless, it was no easy matter to grasp the wishes of the poor old woman. Therese alone possessed this faculty. She communicated fairly well with this walled-up brain, still alive, but buried in a lifeless frame. What was passing within this wretched creature, just sufficiently alive to be present at the events of life, without taking part in them? She saw and heard, she no doubt reasoned in a distinct and clear manner. But she was without gesture and voice to express the thoughts originating in her mind. Her ideas were perhaps choking her, and yet she could not raise a hand, nor open her mouth, even though one of her movements or words should decide the destiny of the world.

Her mind resembled those of the living buried by mistake, who awaken in the middle of the night in the earth, three or four yards below the surface of the ground. They shout, they struggle, and people pass over them without hearing their atrocious lamentations.

Laurent frequently gazed at Madame Raquin, his lips pressed together, his hands stretched out on his knees, putting all his life into his sparkling and swiftly moving eyes. And he said to himself:

"Who knows what she may be thinking of all alone? Some cruel drama must be passing within this inanimate frame."

Laurent made a mistake. Madame Raquin was happy, happy at the care and affection bestowed on her by her dear children. She had always dreamed of ending in this gentle way, amidst devotedness and caresses. Certainly she would have been pleased to have preserved her speech, so as to be able to thank the friends who assisted her to die in peace. But she accepted her condition without rebellion. The tranquil and retired life she had always led, the sweetness of her character, prevented her feeling too acutely the suffering of being mute and unable to make a movement. She had entered second childhood. She passed days without weariness, gazing before her, and musing on the past. She even tasted the charm of remaining very good in her armchair, like a little girl.

Each day the sweetness and brightness of her eyes became more penetrating. She had reached the point of making them perform the duties of a hand or mouth, in asking for what she required and in expressing her thanks. In this way she replaced the organs that were wanting, in a most peculiar and charming manner. Her eyes, in the centre of her flabby and grimacing face, were of celestial beauty.

Since her twisted and inert lips could no longer smile, she smiled with adorable tenderness, by her looks; moist beams and rays of dawn issued from her orbits. Nothing was more peculiar than those eyes which laughed like lips in this lifeless countenance. The lower part of the face remained gloomy and wan, while the upper part was divinely lit up. It was particularly for her beloved children that she placed all her gratitude, all the affection of her soul into a simple glance. When Laurent took her in his arms, morning and night, to carry her, she thanked him lovingly by looks full of tender effusion.

She lived thus for weeks, awaiting death, fancying herself sheltered from any fresh misfortune. She thought she had already received her share of suffering. But she was mistaken. One night she was crushed by a frightful blow.

Therese and Laurent might well place her between them, in the full light, but she was no longer sufficiently animated to separate and defend them against their anguish. When they forgot that she was there and could hear and see them, they were seized with folly. Perceiving Camille, they sought to drive him away. Then, in unsteady tones, they allowed the truth to escape them, uttering words that revealed everything to Madame Raquin. Laurent had a sort of attack, during which he spoke like one under the influence of hallucination, and the paralysed woman abruptly understood.

A frightful contraction passed over her face, and she experienced such a shock that Therese thought she was about to bound to her feet and shriek, but she fell backward, rigid as iron. This shock was all the more terrible as it seemed to galvanise a corpse. Sensibility which had for a moment returned, disappeared; the impotent woman remained more crushed and wan than before. Her eyes, usually so gentle, had become dark and harsh, resembling pieces of metal.

Never had despair fallen more rigorously on a being. The sinister truth, like a flash of flame, scorched the eyes of the paralysed woman and penetrated within her with the concussion of a shaft of lightning. Had she been able to rise, to utter the cry of horror that ascended to her throat, and curse the murderers of her son, she would have suffered less. But, after hearing and understanding everything, she was forced to remain motionless and mute, inwardly preserving all the glare of her grief.

It seemed to her that Therese and Laurent had bound her, riveted her to her armchair to prevent her springing up, and that they took atrocious pleasure in repeating to her, after gagging her to stifle her cries—

"We have killed Camille!"

Terror and anguish coursed furiously in her body unable to find an issue. She made superhuman efforts to raise the weight crushing her, to clear her throat and thus give passage to her flood of despair. In vain did she strain her final energy; she felt her tongue cold against her palate, she could not tear herself from death. Cadaverous impotence held her rigid. Her sensations resembled those of a man fallen into lethargy, who is being buried, and who, bound by the bonds of his own frame, hears the deadened sound of the shovels of mould falling on his head.

The ravages to which her heart was subjected, proved still more terrible. She felt a blow inwardly that completely undid her. Her entire life was afflicted: all her tenderness, all her goodness, all her devotedness had just been brutally upset and trampled under foot. She had led a life of affection and gentleness, and in her last hours, when about to carry to the grave a belief in the delight of a calm life, a voice shouted to her that all was falsehood and all crime.

The veil being rent, she perceived apart from the love and friendship which was all she had hitherto been able to see, a frightful picture of blood and shame. She would have cursed the Almighty had she been able to shout out a blasphemy. Providence had deceived her for over sixty years, by treating her as a gentle, good little girl, by amusing her with lying representations of tranquil joy. And she had remained a child, senselessly believing in a thousand silly things, and unable to see life as it really is, dragging along in the sanguinary filth of passions. Providence was bad; it should have told her the truth before, or have allowed her to continue in her innocence and blindness. Now, it only remained for her to die, denying love, denying friendship, denying devotedness. Nothing existed but murder and lust.

What! Camille had been killed by Therese and Laurent, and they had conceived the crime in shame! For Madame Raquin, there was such a fathomless depth in this thought, that she could neither reason it out, nor grasp it clearly. She experienced but one sensation, that of a horrible disaster; it seemed to her that she was falling into a dark, cold hole. And she said to herself:

"I shall be smashed to pieces at the bottom."

After the first shock, the crime appeared to her so monstrous that it seemed impossible. Then, when convinced of the misbehaviour and murder, by recalling certain little incidents which she had formerly failed to understand, she was afraid of going out of her mind. Therese and Laurent were really the murderers of Camille: Therese whom she had reared, Laurent whom she had loved with the devoted and tender affection of a mother. These thoughts revolved in her head like an immense wheel, accompanied by a deafening noise.

She conjectured such vile details, fathomed such immense hypocrisy, assisting in thought at a double vision so atrocious in irony, that she would have liked to die, mechanical and implacable, pounded her brain with the weight and ceaseless action of a millstone. She repeated to herself:

"It is my children who have killed my child."

And she could think of nothing else to express her despair.

In the sudden change that had come over her heart, she no longer recognised herself. She remained weighed down by the brutal invasion of ideas of vengeance that drove away all the goodness of her life. When she had been thus transformed, all was dark inwardly; she felt the birth of a new being within her frame, a being pitiless and cruel, who would have liked to bite the murderers of her son.

When she had succumbed to the overwhelming stroke of paralysis, when she understood that she could not fly at the throats of Therese and Laurent, whom she longed to strangle, she resigned herself to silence and immobility, and great tears fell slowly from her eyes. Nothing could be more heartrending than this mute and motionless despair. Those tears coursing, one by one, down this lifeless countenance, not a wrinkle of which moved, that inert, wan face which could not weep with its features, and whose eyes alone sobbed, presented a poignant spectacle.

Therese was seized with horrified pity.

"We must put her to bed," said she to Laurent, pointing to her aunt.

Laurent hastened to roll the paralysed woman into her bedroom. Then, as he stooped down to take her in his arms, Madame Raquin hoped that some powerful spring would place her on her feet; and she attempted a supreme effort. The Almighty would not permit Laurent to press her to his bosom; she fully anticipated he would be struck down if he displayed such monstrous impudence. But no spring came into action, and heaven reserved its lightning. Madame Raquin remained huddled up and passive like a bundle of linen. She was grasped, raised and carried along by the assassin; she experienced the anguish of feeling herself feeble and abandoned in the arms of the murderer of Camille. Her head rolled on to the shoulder of Laurent, whom she observed with eyes increased in volume by horror.

"You may look at me," he murmured. "Your eyes will not eat me."

And he cast her brutally on the bed. The impotent old lady fell unconscious on the mattress. Her last thought had been one of terror and disgust. In future, morning and night, she would have to submit to the vile pressure of the arms of Laurent.

CHAPTER XXVII

A shock of terror alone had made the married pair speak, and avow their crime in the presence of Madame Raquin. Neither one nor the other was cruel; they would have avoided such a revelation out of feelings of humanity, had not their own security already made it imperative on their part to maintain silence.

On the ensuing Thursday, they felt particularly anxious. In the morning, Therese inquired of Laurent whether he considered it prudent to leave the paralysed woman in the dining-room during the evening. She knew all and might give the alarm.

"Bah!" replied Laurent, "it is impossible for her to raise her little finger. How can she babble?"

"She will perhaps discover a way to do so," answered Therese. "I have noticed an implacable thought in her eyes since the other evening."

"No," said Laurent. "You see, the doctor told me it was absolutely all over with her. If she ever speaks again it will be in the final death-rattle. She will not last much longer, you may be sure. It would be stupid to place an additional load on our conscience by preventing her being present at the gathering this evening."

Therese shuddered.

"You misunderstand me," she exclaimed. "Oh! You are right. There has been enough crime. I meant to say that we might shut our aunt up in her own room, pretending she was not well, and was sleeping."

"That's it," replied Laurent, "and that idiot Michaud would go straight into the room to see his old friend, notwithstanding. It would be a capital way to ruin us."

He hesitated. He wanted to appear calm, and anxiety gave a tremor to his voice.

"It will be best to let matters take their course," he continued. "These people are as silly as geese. The mute despair of the old woman will certainly teach them nothing. They will never have the least suspicion of the thing, for they are too far away from the truth. Once the ordeal is over, we shall be at ease as to the consequences of our imprudence. All will be well, you will see."

When the guests arrived in the evening, Madame Raquin occupied her usual place, between the stove and table. Therese and Laurent feigned to be in good spirits, concealing their shudders and awaiting, in anguish, the incident that was bound to occur. They had brought the lamp-shade very low down, so that the oilcloth table covering alone was lit up.

The guests engaged in the usual noisy, common-place conversation that invariably preceded the first game of dominoes. Grivet and Michaud did not fail to address the usual questions to the paralysed woman, on the subject of her health, and to give excellent answers to them, as was their custom. After which, the company, without troubling any further about the poor old lady, plunged with delight into the game.

Since Madame Raquin had become aware of the horrible secret, she had been awaiting this evening with feverish impatience. She had gathered together all her remaining strength to denounce the culprits. Up to the last moment, she feared she would not be present at the gathering; she thought Laurent would make her disappear, perhaps kill her, or at least shut her up in her own apartment. When she saw that her niece and nephew allowed her to remain in the dining-room, she experienced lively joy at the thought of attempting to avenge her son.

Aware that her tongue was powerless, she resorted to a new kind of language. With astonishing power of will, she succeeded, in a measure, in galvanising her right hand, in slightly raising it from her knee, where it always lay stretched out, inert; she then made it creep little by little up one of the legs of the table before her, and thus succeeded in placing it on the oilcloth table cover. Then, she feebly agitated the fingers as if to attract attention.

When the players perceived this lifeless hand, white and nerveless, before them, they were exceedingly surprised. Grivet stopped short, with his arm in the air, at the moment when he was about to play the double-six. Since the impotent woman had been struck down, she had never moved her hands.

"Hey! Just look, Therese," cried Michaud. "Madame Raquin is agitating her fingers. She probably wants something."

Therese could not reply. Both she and Laurent had been following the exertion of the paralysed woman, and she was now looking at the hand of her aunt, which stood out wan in the raw light of the lamp, like an avenging hand that was about to speak. The two murderers waited, breathless.

"Of course," said Grivet, "she wants something. Oh! We thoroughly understand one another. She wants to play dominoes. Eh! Isn't it so, dear lady?"

Madame Raquin made a violent sign indicating that she wanted nothing of the kind. She extended one finger, folded up the others with infinite difficulty, and began to painfully trace letters on the table cover. She had barely indicated a stroke or two, when Grivet again exclaimed in triumph:

"I understand; she says I do right to play the double-six."

The impotent woman cast a terrible glance at the old clerk, and returned to the word she wished to write. But Grivet interrupted her at every moment, declaring it was needless, that he understood, and he then brought out some stupidity. Michaud at last made him hold his tongue.

"The deuce! Allow Madame Raquin to speak," said he. "Speak, my old friend."

And he gazed at the oilcloth table cover as if he had been listening. But the fingers of the paralysed woman were growing weary. They had begun the word more than ten times over, and now, in tracing this word, they wandered to right and left. Michaud and Olivier bent forward, and being unable to read, forced the impotent old lady to resume the first letters.

"Ah! Bravo!" exclaimed Olivier, all at once, "I can read it, this time. She has just written your name, Therese. Let me see: '*Therese and——*' Complete the sentence, dear lady."

Therese almost shrieked in anguish. She watched the finger of her aunt gliding over the oilcloth, and it seemed to her that this finger traced her name, and the confession of her crime in letters of fire. Laurent had risen violently, with half a mind to fling himself on the paralysed woman and break her arm. When he saw this hand return to life to reveal the murder of Camille, he thought all was lost, and already felt the weight and frigidity of the knife on the nape of his neck.

Madame Raquin still wrote, but in a manner that became more and more hesitating.

"This is perfect. I can read it very well indeed," resumed Olivier after an instant, and with his eyes on the married pair. "Your aunt writes your two names: '*Therese and Laurent.*'"

The old lady made sign after sign in the affirmative, casting crushing glances on the murderers. Then she sought to complete the sentence, but her fingers had stiffened, the supreme will that galvanised them, escaped her. She felt the paralysis slowly descending her arm and again grasping her wrist. She hurried on, and traced another word.

Old Michaud read out in a loud voice:

"Therese and Laurent have—"

And Olivier inquired:

"What have your dear children?"

The murderers, seized with blind terror, were on the point of completing the sentence aloud. They contemplated the avenging hand with fixed and troubled eyes, when, all at once this hand became convulsed, and flattened out on the table. It slipped down and fell on the knee of the impotent woman like a lump of inanimate flesh and bone. The paralysis had returned and arrested the punishment. Michaud and Olivier sat down again disappointed, while Therese and Laurent experienced such keen joy that they felt like fainting under the influence of the sudden rush of blood that beat in their bosoms.

Grivet who felt vexed at not having been believed on trust, thought the moment had arrived to regain his infallibility, by completing the unfinished sentence. While every one was endeavouring to supply the missing words, he exclaimed:

"It is quite clear. I can read the whole phrase in the eyes of the lady. It is not necessary for her to write on the table to make me understand; a mere look suffices. She means to say:

"Therese and Laurent have been very kind to me."

Grivet, on this occasion, had cause to be proud of his imagination, for all the company were of his opinion; and the guests began to sing the praises of the married couple, who were so good for the poor lady.

"It is certain," old Michaud gravely remarked, "that Madame Raquin wishes to bear testimony to the tender affection her children lavish on her, and this does honour to the whole family."

Then, taking up his dominoes again, he added:

"Come, let us continue. Where were we? Grivet was about to play the double-six, I think."

Grivet played the double six, and the stupid, monotonous game went on.

The paralysed woman, cut up by frightful despair, looked at her hand, which had just betrayed her. She felt it as heavy as lead, now; never would she be able to raise it again. Providence would not permit

Camille to be avenged. It withdrew from his mother the only means she had of making known the crime to which he had fallen a victim. And the wretched woman said to herself that she was now only fit to go and join her child underground. She lowered her lids, feeling herself, henceforth, useless, and with the desire of imagining herself already in the darkness of the tomb.

CHAPTER XXVIII

For two months, Therese and Laurent had been struggling in the anguish of their union. One suffered through the other. Then hatred slowly gained them, and they ended by casting angry glances at one another, full of secret menace.

Hatred was forced to come. They had loved like brutes, with hot passion, entirely sanguineous. Then, amidst the enervation of their crime, their love had turned to fright, and their kisses had produced a sort of physical terror. At present, amid the suffering which marriage, which life in common imposed on them, they revolted and flew into anger.

It was a bitter hatred, with terrible outbursts. They felt they were in the way of one another, and both inwardly said that they would lead a tranquil existence were they not always face to face. When in presence of each other, it seemed as if an enormous weight were stifling them, and they would have liked to remove this weight, to destroy it. Their lips were pinched, thoughts of violence passed in their clear eyes, and a craving beset them to devour one another.

In reality, one single thought tormented them: they were irritated at their crime, and in despair at having for ever troubled their lives. Hence all their anger and hatred. They felt the evil incurable, that they would suffer for the murder of Camille until death, and this idea of perpetual suffering exasperated them. Not knowing whom to strike, they turned in hatred on one another.

They would not openly admit that their marriage was the final punishment of the murder; they refused to listen to the inner voice that shouted out the truth to them, displaying the story of their life before their eyes. And yet, in the fits of rage that bestirred them, they both saw clearly to the bottom of their anger, they were aware it was the furious impulse of their egotistic nature that had urged them to murder in order to satisfy their desire, and that they had only found in assassination, an afflicted and intolerable existence. They recollected the past, they knew that their mistaken hopes of lust and peaceful happiness had alone brought them to remorse. Had they been able to embrace one another in peace, and live in joy, they would not have mourned Camille, they would have fattened on their crime. But their bodies had rebelled, refusing marriage, and they inquired of themselves, in terror, where horror and disgust would lead them. They only perceived a future that would be horrible in pain, with a sinister and violent end.

Then, like two enemies bound together, and who were making violent efforts to release themselves from this forced embrace, they strained their muscles and nerves, stiffening their limbs without succeeding in releasing themselves. At last understanding that they would never be able to escape from their clasp, irritated by the cords cutting into their flesh, disgusted at their contact, feeling their discomfort increase at every moment, forgetful, and unable to bear their bonds a moment longer, they addressed outrageous reproaches to one another, in the hope of suffering loss, of dressing the wounds they inflicted on themselves, by cursing and deafening each other with their shouts and accusations.

A quarrel broke out every evening. It looked as though the murderers sought opportunities to become exasperated so as to relax their rigid nerves. They watched one another, sounded one another with glances, examined the wounds of one another, discovering the raw parts, and taking keen pleasure in causing each other to yell in pain. They lived in constant irritation, weary of themselves, unable to support a word, a gesture or a look, without suffering and frenzy. Both their beings were prepared for violence; the least display of impatience, the most ordinary contrariety increased immoderately in their disordered organism, and all at once, took the form of brutality. A mere nothing raised a storm that lasted until the morrow. A plate too warm, an open window, a denial, a simple observation, sufficed to drive them into regular fits of madness.

In the course of the discussion, they never failed to bring up the subject of the drowned man. From sentence to sentence they came to mutual reproaches about this drowning business at Saint-Ouen, casting the crime in the face of one another. They grew excited to the pitch of fury, until one felt like murdering the other. Then ensued atrocious scenes of choking, blows, abominable cries, shameless brutalities. As a rule, Therese and Laurent became exasperated, in this manner, after the evening meal. They shut themselves up in the dining-room, so that the sound of their despair should not be heard. There, they could devour one another at ease. At the end of this damp apartment, of this sort of vault, lighted by the yellow beams of the lamp, the tone of their voices took harrowing sharpness, amidst the silence and tranquillity of the atmosphere. And they did not cease until exhausted with fatigue; then only could they go and enjoy a few hours' rest. Their quarrels became, in a measure, necessary to them—a means of procuring a few hours' rest by stupefying their nerves.

Madame Raquin listened. She never ceased to be there, in her armchair, her hands dangling on her knees, her head straight, her face mute. She heard everything, and not a shudder ran through her lifeless frame. Her eyes rested on the murderers with the most acute fixedness. Her martyrdom must have been atrocious. She thus learned, detail by detail, all the events that had preceded and followed the murder of Camille. Little by little her ears became polluted with an account of the filth and crimes of those whom she had called her children.

These quarrels of the married couple placed her in possession of the most minute circumstances connected with the murder, and spread out, one by one, before her terrified mind, all the episodes of the horrible adventure. As she went deeper into this sanguinary filth, she pleaded in her mind for mercy, at times, she fancied she was touching the bottom of the infamy, and still she had to descend lower. Each night, she learnt some new detail. The frightful story continued to expand before her. It seemed like being lost in an interminable dream of horror. The first avowal had been brutal and crushing, but she suffered more from these repeated blows, from these small facts which the husband and wife allowed to escape them in their fits of anger, and which lit up the crime with sinister rays. Once a day, this mother heard the account of the murder of her son; and, each day this account became more horrifying, more replete with detail, and was shouted into her ears with greater cruelty and uproar.

On one occasion, Therese, taken aback with remorse, at the sight of this wan countenance, with great tears slowly coursing down its cheeks, pointed out her aunt to Laurent, beseeching him with a look to hold his tongue.

"Well, what of it? Leave me alone!" exclaimed the latter in a brutal tone, "you know very well that she cannot give us up. Am I more happy than she is? We have her cash, I have no need to constrain myself."

The quarrel continued, bitter and piercing, and Camille was killed over again. Neither Therese nor Laurent dared give way to the thoughts of pity that sometimes came over them, and shut the paralysed woman in her bedroom, when they quarrelled, so as to spare her the story of the crime. They were afraid of beating one another to death, if they failed to have this semi-corpse between them. Their pity yielded to cowardice. They imposed ineffable sufferings on Madame Raquin because they required her presence to protect them against their hallucinations.

All their disputes were alike, and led to the same accusations. As soon as one of them accused the other of having killed this man, there came a frightful shock.

One night, at dinner, Laurent who sought a pretext for becoming irritable, found that the water in the decanter was lukewarm. He declared that tepid water made him feel sick, and that he wanted it fresh.

"I was unable to procure any ice," Therese answered dryly.

"Very well, I will deprive myself of drinking," retorted Laurent.

"This water is excellent," said she.

"It is warm, and has a muddy taste," he answered. "It's like water from the river."

"Water from the river?" repeated Therese.

And she burst out sobbing. A juncture of ideas had just occurred in her mind.

"Why do you cry?" asked Laurent, who foresaw the answer, and turned pale.

"I cry," sobbed the young woman, "I cry because—you know why—Oh! Great God! Great God! It was you who killed him."

"You lie!" shouted the murderer vehemently, "confess that you lie. If I threw him into the Seine, it was you who urged me to commit the murder."

"I! I!" she exclaimed.

"Yes, you! Don't act the ignorant," he replied, "don't compel me to force you to tell the truth. I want you to confess your crime, to take your share in the murder. It will tranquillise and relieve me."

"But *I* did not drown Camille," she pleaded.

"Yes, you did, a thousand times yes!" he shouted. "Oh! You feign astonishment and want of memory. Wait a moment, I will recall your recollections."

Rising from table, he bent over the young woman, and with crimson countenance, yelled in her face:

"You were on the river bank, you remember, and I said to you in an undertone: 'I am going to pitch him into the water.' Then you agreed to it, you got into the boat. You see that we murdered him together."

"It is not true," she answered. "I was crazy, I don't know what I did, but I never wanted to kill him. You alone committed the crime."

These denials tortured Laurent. As he had said, the idea of having an accomplice relieved him. Had he dared, he would have attempted to prove to himself that all the horror of the murder fell upon Therese. He more than once felt inclined to beat the young woman, so as to make her confess that she was the more guilty of the two.

He began striding up and down, shouting and raving, followed by the piercing eyes of Madame Raquin.

"Ah! The wretch! The wretch!" he stammered in a choking voice, "she wants to drive me mad. Look, did you not come up to my room one evening, did you not intoxicate me with your caresses to persuade me to rid you of your husband? You told me, when I visited you here, that he displeased you, that he had the odour of a sickly child. Did I think of all this three years ago? Was I a rascal? I was leading the peaceful existence of an upright man, doing no harm to anybody. I would not have killed a fly."

"It was you who killed Camille," repeated Therese with such desperate obstinacy that she made Laurent lose his head.

"No, it was you, I say it was you," he retorted with a terrible burst of rage. "Look here, don't exasperate me, or if you do you'll suffer for it. What, you wretch, have you forgotten everything? You who maddened me with your caresses! Confess that it was all a calculation in your mind, that you hated Camille, and that you had wanted to kill him for a long time. No doubt you took me as a sweetheart, so as to drive me to put an end to him."

"It is not true," said she. "What you relate is monstrous. You have no right to reproach me with my weakness towards you. I can speak in regard to you, as you speak of me. Before I knew you, I was a good woman, who never wronged a soul. If I drove you mad, it was you made me madder still. Listen Laurent, don't let us quarrel. I have too much to reproach you with."

"What can you reproach me with?" he inquired.

"No, nothing," she answered. "You did not save me from myself, you took advantage of my surrender, you chose to spoil my life. I forgive you all that. But, in mercy, do not accuse me of killing Camille. Keep your crime for yourself. Do not seek to make me more terrified than I am already."

Laurent raised his hand to strike her in the face.

"Beat me, I prefer that," said she, "I shall suffer less."

And she advanced her head. But he restrained himself, and taking a chair, sat down beside her.

"Listen," he began in a voice that he endeavoured to render calm, "it is cowardly to refuse to take your share in the crime. You know perfectly well that as we did the deed together, you know you are as guilty as I am. Why do you want to make my load heavier, by saying you are innocent? If you were so, you would not have consented to marry me. Just recall what passed during the two years following the murder. Do you want a proof? If so I will go and relate everything to the Public Prosecutor, and you will see whether we are not both condemned."

They shuddered, and Therese resumed:

"Men may, perhaps, condemn me, but Camille knows very well that you did everything. He does not torment me at night as he does you."

"Camille leaves me in peace," said Laurent, pale and trembling, "it is you who see him before you in your nightmares. I have heard you shout out."

"Don't say that," angrily exclaimed the young woman. "I have never shouted out. I don't wish the spectre to appear. Oh! I understand, you want to drive it away from yourself. I am innocent, I am innocent!"

They looked at one another in terror, exhausted with fatigue, fearing they had evoked the corpse of the drowned man. Their quarrels invariably ended in this way; they protested their innocence, they sought to deceive themselves, so as to drive away their bad dreams. They made constant efforts, each in turn, to reject the responsibility of the crime, defending themselves as though they were before a judge and jury, and accusing one another.

The strangest part of this attitude was that they did not succeed in duping themselves by their oaths. Both had a perfect recollection of all the circumstances connected with the murder, and their eyes avowed what their lips denied.

Their falsehoods were puerile, their affirmations ridiculous. It was the wordy dispute of two wretches who lied for the sake of lying, without succeeding in concealing from themselves that they did so. Each took the part of accuser in turn, and although the prosecution they instituted against one another proved barren of result, they began it again every evening with cruel tenacity.

They were aware that they would prove nothing, that they would not succeed in effacing the past, and still they attempted this task, still they returned to the charge, spurred on by pain and terror, vanquished in advance by overwhelming reality. The sole advantage they derived from their disputes, consisted in producing a tempest of words and cries, and the riot occasioned in this manner momentarily deafened them.

And all the time their anger lasted, all the time they were accusing one another, the paralysed woman never ceased to gaze at them. Ardent joy sparkled in her eyes, when Laurent raised his broad hand above the head of Therese.

CHAPTER XXIX

Matters now took a different aspect. Therese, driven into a corner by fright, not knowing which way to turn for a consoling thought, began to weep aloud over the drowned man, in the presence of Laurent.

She abruptly became depressed, her overstrained nerves relaxed, her unfeeling and violent nature softened. She had already felt compassionate in the early days of her second marriage, and this feeling now returned, as a necessary and fatal reaction.

When the young woman had struggled with all her nervous energy against the spectre of Camille, when she had lived in sullen irritation for several months up in arms against her sufferings, seeking to get the better of them by efforts of will, she all at once experienced such extraordinary lassitude that she yielded vanquished. Then, having become a woman again, even a little girl, no longer feeling the strength to stiffen herself, to stand feverishly erect before her terror, she plunged into pity, into tears and regret, in the hope of finding some relief. She sought to reap advantage from her weakness of body and mind. Perhaps the drowned man, who had not given way to her irritation, would be more unbending to her tears.

Her remorse was all calculation. She thought that this would no doubt be the best way to appease and satisfy Camille. Like certain devotees, who fancy they will deceive the Almighty, and secure pardon by praying with their lips, and assuming the humble attitude of penitence, Therese displayed humility, striking her chest, finding words of repentance, without having anything at the bottom of her heart save fear and cowardice. Besides, she experienced a sort of physical pleasure in giving way in this manner, in feeling feeble and undone, in abandoning herself to grief without resistance.

She overwhelmed Madame Raquin with her tearful despair. The paralysed woman became of daily use to her. She served as a sort of praying-desk, as a piece of furniture in front of which Therese could fearlessly confess her faults and plead for forgiveness. As soon as she felt inclined to cry, to divert herself by sobbing, she knelt before the impotent old lady, and there, wailing and choking, performed to her alone a scene of remorse which weakened but relieved her.

"I am a wretch," she stammered, "I deserve no mercy. I deceived you, I drove your son to his death. Never will you forgive me. And yet, if you only knew how I am rent by remorse, if you only knew how I suffer, perhaps you would have pity. No, no pity for me. I should like to die here at your feet, overwhelmed by shame and grief."

She spoke in this manner for hours together, passing from despair to hope, condemning and then pardoning herself; she assumed the voice, brief and plaintive in turn, of a little sick girl; she flattened herself on the ground and drew herself up again, acting upon all the ideas of humility and pride, of repentance and revolt that entered her head. Sometimes even, forgetting she was on her knees before Madame Raquin, she continued her monologue as in a dream. When she had made herself thoroughly giddy with her own words, she rose staggering and dazed, to go down to the shop in a calmer frame of mind, no longer fearing to burst into sobs before her customers. When she again felt inclined for remorse, she ran upstairs and knelt at the feet of the impotent woman. This scene was repeated ten times a day.

Therese never reflected that her tears, and display of repentance must impose ineffable anguish on her aunt. The truth was that if she had desired to invent a torment to torture Madame Raquin, it would not have been possible to have found a more frightful one than the comedy of remorse she performed before her. The paralysed woman could see the egotism concealed beneath these effusions of grief. She suffered horribly from these long monologues which she was compelled to listen to at every instant, and which always brought the murder of Camille before her eyes. She could not pardon, she never departed from the implacable thought of vengeance that her impotency rendered more keen, and all day long she had to listen to pleas for pardon, and to humble and cowardly prayers.

She would have liked to give an answer; certain sentences of her niece brought crushing refusals to her lips, but she had to remain mute and allow Therese to plead her cause without once interrupting her. The impossibility of crying out and stopping her ears caused her inexpressible torture. The words of the young woman entered her mind, slow and plaintive, as an irritating ditty. At first, she fancied the murderers inflicted this kind of torture on her out of sheer diabolical cruelty. Her sole means of defence was to close her eyes, as soon as her niece knelt before her, then although she heard, she did not see her.

Therese, at last, had the impudence to kiss her aunt. One day, in a fit of repentance, she feigned she had perceived a gleam of mercy in the eyes of the paralysed woman; and she dragged herself along on her knees, she raised herself up, exclaiming in a distracted tone:

"You forgive me! You forgive me!"

Then she kissed the forehead and cheeks of the poor old creature, who was unable to throw her head backward so as to avoid the embrace. The cold skin on which Therese placed her lips, caused her violent disgust. She fancied this disgust, like the tears of remorse, would be an excellent remedy to appease her nerves; and she continued to kiss the impotent old woman daily, by way of penitence, and also to relieve herself.

"Oh! How good you are!" she sometimes exclaimed. "I can see my tears have touched you. Your eyes are full of pity. I am saved."

Then she smothered her with caresses, placing the head of the infirm old lady on her knees, kissing her hands, smiling at her happily, and attending to all her requirements with a display of passionate affection. After a time, she believed in the reality of this comedy, she imagined she had obtained the pardon of Madame Raquin, and spoke of nothing but the delight she experienced at having secured her pardon.

This was too much for the paralysed woman. It almost killed her. At the kisses of her niece, she again felt that sensation of bitter repugnance and rage which came over her, morning and night, when Laurent took her in his arms to lift her up, or lay her down. She was obliged to submit to the disgusting caresses of the wretch who had betrayed and killed her son. She could not even use her hand to wipe away the kisses that this woman left on her cheeks; and, for hours and hours together, she felt these kisses burning her.

She became the doll of the murderers of Camille, a doll that they dressed, that they turned to right and left, and that they made use of according to their requirements and whims. She remained inert in their hands, as if she had been a lay-figure, and yet she lived, and became excited and indignant at the least contact with Therese or Laurent.

What particularly exasperated her was the atrocious mockery of the young woman, who pretended she perceived expressions of mercy in her eyes, when she would have liked to have brought down fire from heaven on the head of the criminal. She frequently made supreme efforts to utter a cry of protestation, and loaded her looks with hatred. But Therese, who found it answered her purpose to repeat twenty times a day that she was pardoned, redoubled her caresses, and would see nothing. So the paralysed woman had to accept the thanks and effusions that her heart repelled. Henceforth, she lived in a state of bitter but powerless irritation, face to face with her yielding niece who displayed adorable acts of tenderness to recompense her for what she termed her heavenly goodness.

When Therese knelt before Madame Raquin, in the presence of her husband, he brutally brought her to her feet.

"No acting," said he. "Do I weep, do I prostrate myself? You do all this to trouble me."

The remorse of Therese caused him peculiar agitation. His suffering increased now that his accomplice dragged herself about him, with eyes red by weeping, and supplicating lips. The sight of this living example of regret redoubled his fright and added to his uneasiness. It was like an everlasting reproach wandering through the house. Then he feared that repentance would one day drive his wife to reveal everything. He would have preferred her to remain rigid and threatening, bitterly defending herself against his accusations. But she had changed her tactics. She now readily recognised the share she had taken in the crime. She even accused herself. She had become yielding and timid, and starting from this point implored redemption with ardent humility. This attitude irritated Laurent, and every evening the quarrels of the couple became more afflicting and sinister.

"Listen to me," said Therese to her husband, "we are very guilty. We must repent if we wish to enjoy tranquillity. Look at me. Since I have been weeping I am more peaceable. Imitate me. Let us say together that we are justly punished for having committed a horrible crime."

"Bah!" roughly answered Laurent, "you can say what you please. I know you are deucedly clever and hypocritical. Weep, if that diverts you. But I must beg you not to worry me with your tears."

"Ah!" said she, "you are bad. You reject remorse. You are cowardly. You acted as a traitor to Camille."

"Do you mean to say that I alone am guilty?" he inquired.

"No," she replied, "I do not say that. I am guilty, more guilty than you are. I ought to have saved my husband from your hands. Oh! I am aware of all the horror of my fault. But I have sought pardon, and I have succeeded, Laurent, whereas you continue to lead a disconsolate life. You have not even had the feeling to spare my poor aunt the sight of your vile anger. You have never even addressed a word of regret to her."

And she embraced Madame Raquin, who shut her eyes. She hovered round her, raising the pillow that propped up her head, and showing her all kinds of attention. Laurent was infuriated.

"Oh, leave her alone," he cried. "Can't you see that your services, and the very sight of you are odious to her. If she could lift her hand she would slap your face."

The slow and plaintive words of his wife, and her attitudes of resignation, gradually drove him into blinding fits of anger. He understood her tactics; she no longer wished to be at one with him, but to set herself apart wrapped in her regret, so as to escape the clasp of the drowned man. And, at moments, he said to himself that she had perhaps taken the right path, that tears might cure her of her terror, and he shuddered at the thought of having to suffer, and contend with fright alone.

He also would have liked to repent, or at least to have performed the comedy of repentance, to see what effect it would have. Unable to find the sobs and necessary words, he flung himself into violence again, stirring up Therese so as to irritate her and lead her back with him to furious madness. But the young woman took care to remain inert, to answer his cries of anger by tearful submission, and to meet his coarseness by a proportionate display of humility and repentance. Laurent was thus gradually driven to fury. To crown his irritation, Therese always ended with the panegyric of Camille so as to display the virtues of the victim.

"He was good," said she, "and we must have been very cruel to assail such a warm-hearted man who had never a bad thought."

"He was good, yes, I know," jeered Laurent. "You mean to say he was a fool. You must have forgotten! You pretended you were irritated at the slightest thing he said, that he could not open his mouth without letting out some stupidity."

"Don't jeer," said Therese. "It only remains for you to insult the man you murdered. You know nothing about the feelings of a woman, Laurent; Camille loved me and I loved him."

"You loved him! Ah! Really what a capital idea," exclaimed Laurent. "And no doubt it was because you loved your husband, that you took me as a sweetheart. I remember one day when we were together, that you told me Camille disgusted you, when you felt the end of your fingers enter his flesh as if it were soft clay. Oh! I know why you loved me.

You required more vigorous arms than those of that poor devil."

"I loved him as a sister," answered Therese. "He was the son of my benefactress. He had all the delicate feelings of a feeble man. He showed himself noble and generous, serviceable and loving. And we killed him, good God! good God!"

She wept, and swooned away. Madame Raquin cast piercing glances at her, indignant to hear the praise of Camille sung by such a pair of lips. Laurent who was unable to do anything against this overflow of tears, walked to and fro with furious strides, searching in his head for some means to stifle the remorse of Therese.

All the good he heard said of his victim ended by causing him poignant anxiety. Now and again he let himself be caught by the heartrending accents of his wife. He really believed in the virtues of Camille, and his terror redoubled. But what tried his patience beyond measure was the comparison that the widow of the drowned man never failed to draw between her first and second husband, and which was all to the advantage of the former.

"Well! Yes," she cried, "he was better than you. I would sooner he were alive now, and you in his place underground."

Laurent first of all shrugged his shoulders.

"Say what you will," she continued, becoming animated, "although I perhaps failed to love him in his lifetime, yet I remember all his good qualities now, and do love him. Yes, I love him and hate you, do you hear? For you are an assassin."

"Will you hold your tongue?" yelled Laurent.

"And he is a victim," she went on, notwithstanding the threatening attitude of her husband, "an upright man killed by a rascal. Oh! I am not afraid of you. You know well enough that you are a miserable wretch, a brute of a man without a heart, and without a soul. How can you expect me to love you, now that you are reeking with the blood of Camille? Camille was full of tenderness for me, and I would kill you, do you hear, if that could bring him to life again, and give me back his love."

"Will you hold your tongue, you wretch?" shouted Laurent.

"Why should I hold my tongue?" she retorted. "I am speaking the truth. I would purchase forgiveness at the price of your blood. Ah! How I weep, and how I suffer! It is my own fault if a scoundrel, such as you, murdered my husband. I must go, one of these nights, and kiss the ground where he rests. That will be my final rapture."

Laurent, beside himself, rendered furious by the atrocious pictures that Therese spread out before his eyes, rushed upon her, and threw her down, menacing her with his uplifted fist.

"That's it," she cried, "strike me, kill me! Camille never once raised his hand to me, but you are a monster."

And Laurent, spurred on by what she said, shook her with rage, beat her, bruised her body with his clenched fists. In two instances he almost strangled her. Therese yielded to his blows. She experienced keen delight in being struck, delivering herself up, thrusting her body forward, provoking her husband in every way, so that he might half kill her again. This was another remedy for her suffering. She slept better at night when she had been thoroughly beaten in the evening. Madame Raquin enjoyed exquisite pleasure, when Laurent dragged her niece along the floor in this way, belabouring her with thumps and kicks.

The existence of the assassin had become terrible since the day when Therese conceived the infernal idea of feeling remorse and of mourning Camille aloud. From that moment the wretch lived everlastingly with his victim. At every hour, he had to listen to his wife praising and regretting her first husband. The least incident became a pretext: Camille did this, Camille did that, Camille had such and such qualities, Camille loved in such and such a way.

It was always Camille! Ever sad remarks bewailing his death. Therese had recourse to all her spitefulness to render this torture, which she inflicted on Laurent so as to shield her own self, as cruel as possible. She went into details, relating a thousand insignificant incidents connected with her youth, accompanied by sighs and expressions of regret, and in this manner, mingled the remembrance of the drowned man with every action of her daily life.

The corpse which already haunted the house, was introduced there openly. It sat on the chairs, took its place at table, extended itself on the bed, making use of the various articles of furniture, and of the objects lying about hither and thither. Laurent could touch nothing, not a fork, not a brush, without Therese making him feel that Camille had touched it before him.

The murderer being ceaselessly thrust, so to say, against the man he had killed, ended by experiencing a strange sensation that very nearly drove him out of his mind. By being so constantly compared to

Camille, by making use of the different articles Camille had used, he imagined he was Camille himself, that he was identical with his victim. Then, with his brain fit to burst, he blew at his wife to make her hold her tongue, so as to no longer hear the words that drove him frantic. All their quarrels now ended in blows.

CHAPTER XXX

A time came when Madame Raquin, in order to escape the sufferings she endured, thought of starving herself to death. She had reached the end of her courage, she could no longer support the martyrdom that the presence of the two murderers imposed on her, she longed to find supreme relief in death. Each day her anguish grew more keen, when Therese embraced her, and when Laurent took her in his arms to carry her along like a child. She determined on freeing herself from these clasps and caresses that caused her such horrible disgust. As she had not sufficient life left within her to permit of her avenging her son, she preferred to be entirely dead, and to leave naught in the hands of the assassins but a corpse that could feel nothing, and with which they could do as they pleased.

For two days she refused all nourishment, employing her remaining strength to clench her teeth or to eject anything that Therese succeeded in introducing into her mouth. Therese was in despair. She was asking herself at the foot of which post she should go to weep and repent, when her aunt would be no longer there. She kept up an interminable discourse to prove to Madame Raquin that she should live. She wept, she even became angry, bursting into her former fits of rage, opening the jaw of the paralysed woman as you open that of an animal which resists. Madame Raquin held out, and an odious scene ensued.

Laurent remained absolutely neutral and indifferent. He was astonished at the efforts of Therese to prevent the impotent old woman committing suicide. Now that the presence of the old lady had become useless to them he desired her death. He would not have killed her, but as she wished to die, he did not see the use of depriving her of the means to do so.

"But, let her be!" he shouted to his wife. "It will be a good riddance. We shall, perhaps, be happier when she is no longer here."

This remark repeated several times in the hearing of Madame Raquin, caused her extraordinary emotion. She feared that the hope expressed by Laurent might be realised, and that after her death the couple would enjoy calm and happiness. And she said to herself that it would be cowardly to die, that she had no right to go away before she had seen the end of the sinister adventure. Then, only, could she descend into darkness, to say to Camille:

"You are avenged."

The idea of suicide became oppressive, when she all at once reflected that she would sink into the grave ignorant as to what had happened to the two murderers of her son. There, she would lie in the cold and silent earth, eternally tormented by uncertainty concerning the punishment of her tormentors. To thoroughly enjoy the slumber of death, she must be hushed to rest by the sweet delight of vengeance, she must carry away with her a dream of satisfied hatred, a dream that would last throughout eternity. So she took the food her niece presented to her, and consented to live on.

Apart from this, it was easy for her to perceive that the climax could not be far off. Each day the position of the married couple became more strained and unbearable. A crash that would smash everything was imminent. At every moment, Therese and Laurent started up face to face in a more threatening manner. It was no longer at nighttime, alone, that they suffered from their intimacy; entire days were passed amidst anxiety and harrowing shocks. It was one constant scene of pain and terror. They lived in a perfect pandemonium, fighting, rendering all they did and said bitter and cruel, seeking to fling one another to the bottom of the abyss which they felt beneath their feet, and falling into it together.

Ideas of separation had, indeed, occurred to both of them. Each had thought of flight, of seeking some repose far from this Arcade of the Pont Neuf where the damp and filth seemed adapted to their desolated life. But they dared not, they could not run away. It seemed impossible for them to avoid reviling each other, to avoid remaining there to suffer and cause pain. They proved obstinate in their hatred and cruelty. A sort of repulsion and attraction separated and kept them together at the same time. They behaved in the identical manner of two persons who, after quarrelling, wish to part, and who, nevertheless, continue returning to shout out fresh insults at one another.

Moreover, material obstacles stood in the way of flight. What were they to do with the impotent woman? What could be said to the Thursday evening guests? If they fled, these people would, perhaps, suspect something. At this thought, they imagined they were being pursued and dragged to the guillotine. So they remained where they were through cowardice, wretchedly dragging out their lives amidst the horror of their surroundings.

During the morning and afternoon, when Laurent was absent, Therese went from the dining-room to the shop in anxiety and trouble, at a loss to know what to do to fill up the void in her existence that daily became more pronounced. When not kneeling at the feet of Madame Raquin or receiving blows and insults from her husband, she had no occupation. As soon as she was seated alone in the shop, she became dejected, watching with a doltish expression, the people passing through the dirty, dark gallery. She felt ready to die of sadness in the middle of this gloomy vault, which had the odour of a cemetery, and ended by begging Suzanne to come and pass entire days with her, in the hope that the presence of this poor, gentle, pale creature might calm her.

Suzanne accepted her offer with delight; she continued to feel a sort of respectful friendship for Therese, and had long desired to come and work with her, while Olivier was at his office. Bringing her embroidery with her, she took the vacant chair of Madame Raquin behind the counter.

From that day Therese rather neglected her aunt. She went upstairs less frequently to weep on her knees and kiss the deathlike face of the invalid. She had something else to do. She made efforts to listen with interest to the dilatory gossip of Suzanne, who spoke of her home, and of the trivialities of her monotonous life. This relieved Therese of her own thoughts. Sometimes she caught herself paying attention to nonsense that brought a bitter smile to her face.

By degrees, she lost all her customers. Since her aunt had been confined to her armchair upstairs, she had let the shop go from bad to worse, abandoning the goods to dust and damp. A smell of mildew hung in the atmosphere, spiders came down from the ceiling, the floor was but rarely swept.

But what put the customers to flight was the strange way in which Therese sometimes welcomed them. When she happened to be upstairs, receiving blows from Laurent or agitated by a shock of terror, and the bell at the shop door tinkled imperiously, she had to go down, barely taking time to do up her hair or brush away the tears. On such occasions she served the persons awaiting her roughly; sometimes she even spared herself the trouble of serving, answering from the top of the staircase, that she no longer kept what was asked for. This kind of off-hand behaviour, was not calculated to retain custom.

The little work-girls of the quarter, who were used to the sweet amiability of Madame Raquin, were driven away by the harshness and wild looks of Therese. When the latter took Suzanne with her to keep her company, the defection became complete. To avoid being disturbed in their gossip, the two young woman managed to drive away the few remaining purchasers who visited the shop. Henceforth, the mercery business ceased to bring in a sou towards the household expenses, and it became necessary to encroach on the capital of forty thousand francs and more.

Sometimes, Therese absented herself the entire afternoon. No one knew where she went. Her reason for having Suzanne with her was no doubt partly for the purpose of securing company but also to mind the shop, while she was away. When she returned in the evening, worn out, her eyelids heavy with exhaustion, it was to find the little wife of Olivier still behind the counter, bowed down, with a vague smile on her lips, in the same attitude as she had left her five hours previously.

Therese had a bad fright about five months after her marriage to Laurent. She found out she was pregnant and detested the thought of having a child of Laurent's. She had the fear that she would give birth to a drowned body. She thought that she could feel inside herself a soft, decomposing corpse. No matter what, she had to rid herself of this child. She did not tell Laurent. One day she cruelly provoked him and turned her stomach towards him, hoping to receive a kick. He kicked her and she let him go on kicking her in the stomach until she thought she would die. The next day her wish was fulfilled and she had a miscarriage.

Laurent also led a frightful existence. The days seemed insupportably long; each brought the same anguish, the same heavy weariness which overwhelmed him at certain hours with crushing monotony and regularity. He dragged on his life, terrified every night by the recollections of the day, and the expectation of the morrow. He knew that henceforth, all his days would resemble one another, and bring him equal suffering. And he saw the weeks, months and years gloomily and implacably awaiting him, coming one after the other to fall upon him and gradually smother him.

When there is no hope in the future, the present appears atrociously bitter. Laurent no longer resisted, he became lumpish, abandoning himself to the nothingness that was already gaining possession of his being. Idleness was killing him. In the morning he went out, without knowing where to go, disgusted at the thought of doing what he had done on the previous day, and compelled, in spite of himself, to do it again. He went to his studio by habit, by mania.

This room, with its grey walls, whence he could see naught but a bare square of sky, filled him with mournful sadness. He grovelled on the divan heavy in thought and with pendent arms. He dared not touch a brush. He had made fresh attempts at painting, but only to find on each occasion, the head of Camille appear jeering on the canvas. So as not to go out of his mind, he ended by throwing his colour-box into a corner, and imposing the most absolute idleness on himself. This obligatory laziness weighed upon him terribly.

In the afternoon, he questioned himself in distress to find out what he should do. For half an hour, he remained on the pavement in the Rue Mazarine, thinking and hesitating as to how he could divert himself. He rejected the idea of returning to the studio, and invariably decided on going down the Rue Guenegaud, to walk along the quays. And, until evening, he went along, dazed and seized with sudden shudders whenever he looked at the Seine. Whether in his studio or in the streets, his dejection was the same. The following day he began again. He passed the morning on his divan, and dragged himself along the quays in the afternoon. This lasted for months, and might last for years.

Occasionally Laurent reflected that he had killed Camille so as to do nothing ever afterwards, and now that he did nothing, he was quite astonished to suffer so much. He would have liked to force himself to be happy. He proved to his own satisfaction, that he did wrong to suffer, that he had just attained supreme felicity, consisting in crossing his arms, and that he was an idiot not to enjoy this bliss in peace. But his reasoning exploded in the face of facts. He was constrained to confess, at the bottom of his heart, that this idleness rendered his anguish the more cruel, by leaving him every hour of his life to ponder on the despair and deepen its incurable bitterness. Laziness, that brutish existence which had been his dream, proved his punishment. At moments, he ardently hoped for some occupation to draw him from his thoughts. Then he lost all energy, relapsing beneath the weight of implacable fatality that bound his limbs so as to more surely crush him.

In truth, he only found some relief when beating Therese, at night. This brutality alone relieved him of his enervated anguish.

But his keenest suffering, both physical and moral, came from the bite Camille had given him in the neck. At certain moments, he imagined that this scar covered the whole of his body. If he came to forget the past, he all at once fancied he felt a burning puncture, that recalled the murder both to his frame and mind.

When under the influence of emotion, he could not stand before a looking-glass without noticing this phenomenon which he had so frequently remarked and which always terrified him; the blood flew to his neck, purpling the scar, which then began to gnaw the skin.

This sort of wound that lived upon him, which became active, flushed, and biting at the slightest trouble, frightened and tortured him. He ended by believing that the teeth of the drowned man had planted an insect there which was devouring him. The part of his neck where the scar appeared, seemed to him to no longer belong to his body; it was like foreign flesh that had been stuck in this place, a piece of poisoned meat that was rotting his own muscles.

In this manner, he carried the living and devouring recollection of his crime about with him everywhere. When he beat Therese, she endeavoured to scratch the spot, and sometimes dug her nails into it making him howl with pain. She generally pretended to sob, as soon as she caught sight of the bite, so as to make it more insufferable to Laurent. All her revenge for his brutality, consisted in martyrising him in connection with this bite.

While shaving, he had frequently been tempted to give himself a gash in the neck, so as to make the marks of the teeth of the drowned man disappear. When, standing before the mirror, he raised his chin and perceived the red spot beneath the white lather, he at once flew into a rage, and rapidly brought the razor to his neck, to cut right into the flesh. But the sensations of the cold steel against his skin always brought him to his senses, and caused him to feel so faint that he was obliged to seat himself, and wait until he had recovered sufficient courage to continue shaving.

He only issued from his torpor at night to fall into blind and puerile fits of anger. When tired of quarrelling with Therese and beating her, he would kick the walls like a child, and look for something he could break. This relieved him.

He had a particular dislike for the tabby cat Francois who, as soon as he appeared, sought refuge on the knees of Madame Raquin. If Laurent had not yet killed the animal, it was because he dared not take hold of him. The cat looked at him with great round eyes that were diabolical in their fixedness. He wondered what these eyes which never left him, wanted; and he ended by having regular fits of terror, and imagining all sorts of ridiculous things.

When at table—at no matter what moment, in the middle of a quarrel or of a long silence—he happened, all at once, to look round, and perceive Francois examining him with a harsh, implacable stare, he turned pale and lost his head. He was on the point of saying to the cat:

"Heh! Why don't you speak? Tell me what it is you want with me."

When he could crush his paw or tail, he did so in affrighted joy, the mewing of the poor creature giving him vague terror, as though he heard a human cry of pain. Laurent, in fact, was afraid of Francois, particularly since the latter passed his time on the knees of the impotent old lady, as if in the centre of an impregnable fortress, whence he could with impunity set his eyes on his enemy. The murderer of Camille established a vague resemblance between this irritated animal and the paralysed woman, saying to himself that the cat, like Madame Raquin, must know about the crime and would denounce him, if he ever found a tongue.

At last, one night, Francois looked at Laurent so fixedly, that the latter, irritated to the last pitch, made up his mind to put an end to the annoyance. He threw the window of the dining-room wide open, and advancing to where the cat was seated, grasped him by the skin at the back of the neck. Madame Raquin understood, and two big tears rolled down her cheeks. The cat began to swear, and stiffen himself, endeavouring to turn round and bite the hand that grasped him. But Laurent held fast. He whirled the cat round two or three times in the air, and then sent him flying with all the strength of his arm, against the great dark wall opposite. Francois went flat against it, and breaking his spine, fell upon the glass roof of the arcade. All night the wretched beast dragged himself along the gutter mewing hoarsely, while Madame Raquin wept over him almost as much as she had done over Camille. Therese had an atrocious attack of hysterics, while the wailing of the cat sounded sinisterly, in the gloom below the windows.

Laurent soon had further cause for anxiety. He became alarmed at a certain change he observed in the attitude of his wife.

Therese became sombre and taciturn. She no longer lavished effusions of repentance and grateful kisses on Madame Raquin. In presence of the paralysed woman, she resumed her manner of frigid cruelty and egotistic indifference. It seemed as though she had tried remorse, and finding no relief had turned her attention to another remedy. Her sadness was no doubt due to her inability to calm her life.

She observed the impotent old woman with a kind of disdain, as a useless thing that could no longer even serve her for consolation. She now only bestowed on her the necessary attention to prevent her dying of hunger. From this moment she dragged herself about the house in silence and dejection. She multiplied her absences from the shop, going out as frequently as three and four times a week.

It was this change in her mode of life, that surprised and alarmed Laurent. He fancied that her remorse had taken another form, and was now displayed by this mournful weariness he noticed in her. This weariness seemed to him more alarming than the chattering despair she had overwhelmed him with previously. She no longer spoke, she no longer quarrelled with him, she seemed to consign everything to the depths of her being. He would rather have heard her exhausting her endurance than see her keep in this manner to herself. He feared that one day she would be choking with anguish, and to obtain relief, would go and relate everything to a priest or an examining magistrate.

Then these numerous absences of Therese had frightful significance in his eyes. He thought she went to find a confidant outside, that she was preparing her treason. On two occasions he tried to follow her, and lost her in the streets. He then prepared to watch her again. A fixed idea got into his head: Therese, driven to extremities by suffering, was about to make disclosures, and he must gag her, he must arrest her confession in her throat.

CHAPTER XXXI

One morning, Laurent, instead of going to his studio, took up a position at a wine-shop situated at one of the corners of the Rue Guenegaud, opposite the studio. From there, he began to examine the persons who issued from the passage on to the pavement of the Rue Mazarine. He was watching for Therese. The previous evening, the young woman had mentioned that she intended going out next day and probably would not be home until evening.

Laurent waited fully half an hour. He knew that his wife always went by the Rue Mazarine; nevertheless, at one moment, he remembered that she might escape him by taking the Rue de Seine, and he thought of returning to the arcade, and concealing himself in the corridor of the house. But he determined to retain his seat a little longer, and just as he was growing impatient he suddenly saw Therese come rapidly from the passage.

She wore a light gown, and, for the first time, he noticed that her attire appeared remarkably showy, like a street-walker. She twisted her body about on the pavement, staring provokingly at the men who came along, and raising her skirt, which she clutched in a bunch in her hand, much higher than any respectable woman would have done, in order to display her lace-up boots and stockings. As she went up the Rue Mazarine, Laurent followed her.

It was mild weather, and the young woman walked slowly, with her head thrown slightly backward and her hair streaming down her back. The men who had first of all stared her in the face, turned round to take a back view. She passed into the Rue de l'Ecole de Medecine. Laurent was terrified. He knew that somewhere in this neighbourhood, was a Commissariat of Police, and he said to himself that there could no longer be any doubt as to the intentions of his wife, she was certainly about to denounce him. Then he made up his mind to rush after her, if she crossed the threshold of the commissariat, to implore her, to beat her if necessary, so as to compel her to hold her tongue. At a street corner she looked at a policeman who came along, and Laurent trembled with fright, lest she should stop and speak to him. In terror of being arrested on the spot if he showed himself, he hid in a doorway.

This excursion proved perfect agony. While his wife basked in the sun on the pavement, trailing her skirt with nonchalance and impudence, shameless and unconcerned, he followed behind her, pale and shuddering, repeating that it was all over, that he would be unable to save himself and would be guillotined. Each step he saw her take, seemed to him a step nearer punishment. Fright gave him a sort of blind conviction, and the slightest movement of the young woman added to his certainty. He followed her, he went where she went, as a man goes to the scaffold.

Suddenly on reaching the former Place Saint-Michel, Therese advanced towards a cafe that then formed the corner of the Rue Monsieur-le-Prince. There she seated herself in the centre of a group of women and students, at one of the tables on the pavement, and familiarly shook hands with all this little crowd. Then she called for absinthe.

She seemed quite at ease, chatting with a fair young man who no doubt had been waiting for her some time. Two girls came and leant over the table where she sat, addressing her affectionately in their husky voices. Around her, women were smoking cigarettes, men were embracing women in the open street, before the passers-by, who never even turned their heads. Low words and hoarse laughter reached Laurent, who remained motionless in a doorway on the opposite side of the street.

When Therese had finished her absinthe, she rose, and leaning on the arm of the fair young man, went down the Rue de la Harpe. Laurent followed them as far as the Rue Saint-Andre-des-Arts, where he noticed them enter a lodging-house. He remained in the middle of the street with his eyes on the front of the building. Presently his wife showed herself for an instant at an open window on the second floor, and he fancied he perceived the hands of the pale young man encircling her waist. Then, the window closed with a sharp clang.

Laurent understood. Without waiting a moment longer, he tranquilly took himself off reassured and happy.

"Bah!" said he to himself, as he went towards the quays. "It's better, after all, that she should have a sweetheart. That will occupy her mind, and prevent her thinking of injuring me. She's deucedly more clever than I am."

What astonished him, was that he had not been the first to think of plunging into vice, which might have driven away his terror. But his thoughts had never turned in that direction, and, moreover, he had not the least inclination for riotous living. The infidelity of his wife did not trouble him in the least. He felt no anger at the knowledge that she was in the arms of another man. On the contrary, he seemed to enjoy the idea. He began to think that he had been following the wife of a comrade, and laughed at the cunning trick the woman was playing her husband. Therese had become such a stranger to him, that he no longer felt her alive in his heart. He would have sold her, bound hand and foot, a hundred times over, to purchase calm for one hour.

As he sauntered along, he enjoyed the sudden, delightful reaction that had just brought him from terror to peace. He almost thanked his wife for having gone to a sweetheart, when he thought her on her way to a commissary of police. This adventure had come to an unforeseen end that agreeably surprised him. It distinctly showed him that he had done wrong to tremble, and that he, in his turn, should try vice, in order to see whether such a course would not relieve him by diverting his thoughts.

On returning to the shop in the evening, Laurent decided that he would ask his wife for a few thousand francs, and that he would resort to high-handed measures to obtain them. Reflection told him that vice would be an expensive thing, for a man. He patiently awaited Therese, who had not yet come in. When she arrived, he affected gentleness, and refrained from breathing a word about having followed her in the morning. She was slightly tipsy, and from her ill-adjusted garments, came that unpleasant odour of tobacco and spirits that is met with in public drinking places. Completely exhausted, and with cheeks as pale as death, she advanced at an unsteady gait and with a head quite heavy from the shameless fatigue of the day.

The dinner passed in silence. Therese ate nothing. At dessert Laurent placed his elbows on the table, and flatly asked her for 5,000 francs.

"No," she answered dryly. "If I were to give you a free hand, you'd bring us to beggary. Aren't you aware of our position? We are going as fast as ever we can to the dogs."

"That may be," he quietly resumed. "I don't care a fig, I intend to have money."

"No, a thousand times no!" she retorted. "You left your place, the mercery business is in a very bad way, and the revenue from my marriage portion is not sufficient to maintain us. Every day I encroach on the principal to feed you and give you the one hundred francs a month you wrung from me. You will not get anything beyond that, do you understand? So it's no use asking."

"Just reflect," he replied, "and don't be so silly as to refuse. I tell you I mean to have 5,000 francs, and I shall have them. You'll give them me, in spite of all."

This quiet determination irritated Therese and put the finishing touch to her intoxication.

"Ah! I know what it is," she cried, "you want to finish as you began. We have been keeping you for four years. You only came to us to eat and drink, and since then you've been at our charge. Monsieur does nothing, Monsieur has arranged so as to live at my expense with his arms folded one over the other. No, you shall have nothing, not a sou. Do you want me to tell you what you are? Well then, you are a—"

And she pronounced the word. Laurent began to laugh, shrugging his shoulders. He merely replied:

"You learn some pretty expressions in the company you keep now."

This was the only allusion he ventured to make to the love affairs of Therese. She quickly raised her head, and bitterly replied:

"Anyhow, I don't keep the company of murderers."

Laurent became very pale, and for a moment remained silent, with his eyes fixed on his wife; then, in a trembling voice, he resumed:

"Listen, my girl, don't let us get angry; there is no good in that neither for you nor me. I've lost all courage. We had better come to an understanding if we wish to avoid a misfortune. If I ask you for 5,000 francs it is because I want them; and I will even tell you what I intend to do with them, so as to ensure our tranquillity."

He gave her a peculiar smile, and continued:

"Come, reflect, let me have your last word."

"I have thoroughly made up my mind," answered the young woman, "and it is as I have told you. You shall not have a sou."

Her husband rose violently. She was afraid of being beaten; she crouched down, determined not to give way to blows. But Laurent did not even approach her, he confined himself to telling her in a frigid tone that he was tired of life, and was about to relate the story of the murder to the commissary of police of the quarter.

"You drive me to extremes," said he, "you make my life unbearable. I prefer to have done with it. We shall both be tried and condemned. And there will be an end to it all."

"Do you think you'll frighten me?" shouted his wife. "I am as weary as you are. I'll go to the commissary of police myself, if you don't. Ah! Indeed, I am quite ready to follow you to the scaffold, I'm not a coward like you. Come along, come along with me to the commissary."

She had risen, and was making her way to the staircase.

"That's it," stammered Laurent, "let's go together."

When they were down in the shop they looked at once another, anxious and alarmed. It seemed as though they were riveted to the ground. The few seconds they had taken to run downstairs had suffered to show them, as in a flash, all the consequences of a confession. They saw at the same moment, suddenly and distinctly: gendarmes, prison, assize-court and guillotine. This made them feel faint, and they were tempted to throw themselves on their knees, one before the other, to implore one another to remain, and reveal nothing. Fright and embarrassment kept them motionless and mute for two or three minutes. Therese was the first to make up her mind to speak and give way.

"After all," said she, "I am a great fool to quarrel with you about this money. You will succeed in getting hold of it and squandering it, one day or another. I may just as well give it you at once."

She did not seek to conceal her defeat any further. She seated herself at the counter, and signed a cheque for 5,000 francs, which Laurent was to present to her banker. There was no more question of the commissary of police that evening.

As soon as Laurent had the gold in his pocket, he began to lead a riotous life, drinking to excess, and frequenting women of ill-repute. He slept all day and stayed out all night, in search of violent emotions that would relieve him of reality. But he only succeeded in becoming more oppressed than before. When the company were shouting around him, he heard the great, terrible silence within him; when one of his ladyloves kissed him, when he drained his glass, he found naught at the bottom of his satiety, but heavy sadness.

He was no longer a man for lust and gluttony. His chilled being, as if inwardly rigid, became enervated at the kisses and feasts. Feeling disgusted beforehand, they failed to arouse his imagination or to excite his senses and stomach. He suffered a little more by forcing himself into a dissolute mode of life, and that was all. Then, when he returned home, when he saw Madame Raquin and Therese again, his weariness brought on frightful fits of terror. And he vowed he would leave the house no more, that he would put up with his suffering, so as to become accustomed to it, and be able to conquer it.

For a month Therese lived, like Laurent, on the pavement and in the cafes. She returned daily for a moment, in the evening to feed Madame Raquin and put her to bed, and then disappeared again until the morrow. She and her husband on one occasion were four days without setting eyes on each other. At last, she experienced profound disgust at the life she was leading, feeling that vice succeeded no better with her than the comedy of remorse.

In vain had she dragged through all the lodging-houses in the Latin Quarter, in vain had she led a low, riotous life. Her nerves were ruined. Debauchery ceased to give her a sufficiently violent shock to render her oblivious of the past. She resembled one of those drunkards whose scorched palates remain insensible to the most violent spirits. She had done with lust, and the society of her paramours only worried and wearied her. Then, she quitted them as useless.

She now fell a prey to despondent idleness which kept her at home, in a dirty petticoat, with hair uncombed, and face and hands unwashed. She neglected everything and lived in filth.

When the two murderers came together again face to face, in this manner, after having done their best to get away from each other, they understood that they would no longer have strength to struggle. Debauchery had rejected them, it had just cast them back to their anguish. Once more they were in the dark, damp lodging in the arcade; and, henceforth, were as if imprisoned there, for although they had often attempted to save themselves, never had they been able to sever the sanguinary bond attaching them. They did not even think of attempting a task they regarded as impossible. They found themselves so urged on, so overwhelmed, so securely fastened together by events, that they were conscious all resistance would be ridiculous. They resumed their life in common, but their hatred became furious rage.

The quarrels at night began again. But for that matter, the blows and cries lasted all day long. To hatred distrust was now added, and distrust put the finishing touch to their folly.

They were afraid of each other. The scene that had followed the demand for 5,000 francs, was repeated morning and night. They had the fixed idea that they wanted to give one another up. From that standpoint they did not depart. When either of them said a word, or made a gesture, the other imagined that he or she, as the case might be, intended to go to the commissary of police. Then, they either fought or implored one another to do nothing.

In their anger, they shouted out that they would run and reveal everything, and terrified each other to death. After this they shuddered, they humbled themselves, and promised with bitter tears to maintain silence. They suffered most horribly, but had not the courage to cure themselves by placing a red-hot iron on the wound. If they threatened one another to confess the crime, it was merely to strike terror into each other and drive away the thought, for they would never have had strength to speak and seek peace in punishment.

On more than twenty occasions, they went as far as the door of the commissariat of police, one following the other. Now it was Laurent who wanted to confess the murder, now Therese who ran to give herself up. But they met in the street, and always decided to wait, after an interchange of insults and ardent prayers.

Every fresh attack made them more suspicious and ferocious than before. From morning till night they were spying upon one another. Laurent barely set his foot outside the lodging in the arcade, and if, perchance, he did absent himself, Therese never failed to accompany him. Their suspicions, their fright lest either should confess, brought them together, united them in atrocious intimacy. Never, since their marriage, had they lived so tightly tied together, and never had they experienced such suffering. But, notwithstanding the anguish they imposed on themselves, they never took their eyes off one another. They preferred to endure the most excruciating pain, rather than separate for an hour.

If Therese went down to the shop, Laurent followed, afraid that she might talk to a customer; if Laurent stood in the doorway, observing the people passing through the arcade, Therese placed herself beside him to see that he did not speak to anyone. When the guests were assembled on Thursday evenings, the murderers addressed supplicating glances to each other, listening to one another in terror, one accomplice expecting the other to make some confession, and giving an involving interpretation to sentences only just commenced.

Such a state of warfare could not continue any longer.

Therese and Laurent had both reached the point of pondering on the advisability of extricating themselves from the consequences of their first crime, by committing a second. It became absolutely necessary that one of them should disappear so that the other might enjoy some repose. This reflection came to them both at the same time; both felt the urgent necessity for a separation, and both desired that it should be eternal. The murder that now occurred to their minds, seemed to them natural, fatal and forcibly brought about by the murder of Camille. They did not even turn the matter over in their heads but welcomed the idea as the only means of safety. Laurent determined he would kill Therese because she stood in his way, because she might ruin him by a word, and because she caused him unbearable suffering. Therese made up her mind that she would kill Laurent, for the same reasons.

The firm resolution to commit another murder somewhat calmed them. They formed their plans. But in that respect they acted with feverish excitement, and without any display of excessive prudence. They only thought vaguely of the probable consequences of a murder committed without flight and immunity being ensured. They felt the invincible necessity to kill one another, and yielded to this necessity like furious brutes. They would not have exposed themselves for their first crime, which they had so cleverly concealed, and yet they risked the guillotine, in committing a second, which they did not even attempt to hide.

Here was a contradiction in their conduct that they never so much as caught sight of. Both simply said to themselves that if they succeeded in fleeing, they would go and live abroad, taking all the cash with them. Therese, a fortnight or three weeks before, had drawn from the bank the few thousand francs that remained of her marriage portion, and kept them locked up in a drawer—a circumstance that had not escaped Laurent. The fate of Madame Raquin did not trouble them an instant.

A few weeks previously, Laurent had met one of his old college friends, now acting as dispenser to a famous chemist, who gave considerable attention to toxicology. This friend had shown him over the laboratory where he worked, pointing out to him the apparatus and the drugs.

One night, after he had made up his mind in regard to the murder, and as Therese was drinking a glass of sugar and water before him, Laurent remembered that he had seen in this laboratory a small stoneware flagon, containing prussic acid, and that the young dispenser had spoken to him of the terrible effects of this poison, which strikes the victim down with sudden death, leaving but few traces behind. And Laurent said to himself, that this was the poison he required. On the morrow, succeeding in escaping the vigilance of Therese, he paid his friend a visit, and while he had his back turned, stole the small stoneware flagon.

The same day, Therese took advantage of the absence of Laurent, to send the large kitchen knife, with which they were in the habit of breaking the loaf sugar, and which was very much notched, to be sharpened. When it came back, she hid it in a corner of the sideboard.

CHAPTER XXXII

The following Thursday, the evening party at the Raquins, as the guests continued to term the household of their hosts, was particularly merry. It was prolonged until half-past eleven, and as Grivet withdrew, he declared that he had never passed such a pleasant time.

Suzanne, who was not very well, never ceased talking to Therese of her pain and joy. Therese appeared to listen to her with great interest, her eyes fixed, her lips pinched, her head, at moments, bending forward; while her lowering eyelids cast a cloud over the whole of her face.

Laurent, for his part, gave uninterrupted attention to the tales of old Michaud and Olivier. These gentlemen never paused, and it was only with difficulty that Grivet succeeded in getting in a word edgeways between a couple of sentences of father and son. He had a certain respect for these two men whom he considered good talkers. On that particular evening, a gossip having taken the place of the usual game, he naively blurted out that the conversation of the former commissary of police amused him almost as much as dominoes.

During the four years, or thereabouts, that the Michauds and Grivet had been in the habit of passing the Thursday evenings at the Raquins', they had not once felt fatigued at these monotonous evenings that returned with enervating regularity. Never had they for an instant suspected the drama that was being performed in this house, so peaceful and harmonious when they entered it. Olivier, with the jest of a person connected with the police, was in the habit of remarking that the dining-room savoured of the honest man. Grivet, so as to have his say, had called the place the Temple of Peace.

Latterly, on two or three different occasions, Therese explained the bruises disfiguring her face, by telling the guests she had fallen down. But none of them, for that matter, would have recognised the marks of the fist of Laurent; they were convinced as to their hosts being a model pair, replete with sweetness and love.

The paralysed woman had not made any fresh attempt to reveal to them the infamy concealed behind the dreary tranquillity of the Thursday evenings. An eye-witness of the tortures of the murderers, and foreseeing the crisis which would burst out, one day or another, brought on by the fatal succession of events, she at length understood that there was no necessity for her intervention. And from that moment, she remained in the background allowing the consequences of the murder of Camille, which were to kill the assassins in their turn, to take their course. She only prayed heaven, to grant her sufficient life to enable her to be present at the violent catastrophe she foresaw; her only remaining desire was to feast her eyes on the supreme suffering that would undo Therese and Laurent.

On this particular evening, Grivet went and seated himself beside her, and talked for a long time, he, as usual, asking the questions and supplying the answers himself. But he failed to get even a glance from her. When half-past eleven struck, the guests quickly rose to their feet.

"We are so comfortable with you," said Grivet, "that no one ever thinks of leaving."

"The fact is," remarked Michaud by way of supporting the old clerk, "I never feel drowsy here, although I generally go to bed at nine o'clock."

Olivier thought this a capital opportunity for introducing his little joke.

"You see," said he, displaying his yellow teeth, "this apartment savours of honest people: that is why we are so comfortable here."

Grivet, annoyed at being forestalled, began to declaim with an emphatic gesture:

"This room is the Temple of Peace!"

In the meanwhile, Suzanne, who was putting on her hat, remarked to Therese:

"I will come to-morrow morning at nine o'clock."

"No," hastened to answer the young woman in a strange, troubled tone, "don't come until the afternoon I have an engagement in the morning."

She accompanied the guests into the arcade, and Laurent also went down with a lamp in his hand. As soon as the married couple were alone, both heaved a sigh of relief. They must have been devoured by secret impatience all the evening. Since the previous day they had become more sombre, more anxious in presence of one another. They avoided looking at each other, and returned in silence to the dining-room. Their hands gave slight convulsive twitches, and Laurent was obliged to place the lamp on the table, to avoid letting it fall.

Before putting Madame Raquin to bed they were in the habit of setting the dining-room in order, of preparing a glass of sugar and water for the night, of moving hither and thither about the invalid, until everything was ready.

When they got upstairs on this particular occasion, they sat down an instant with pale lips, and eyes gazing vaguely before them. Laurent was the first to break silence:

"Well! Aren't we going to bed?" he inquired, as if he had just started from a dream.

"Yes, yes, we are going to bed," answered Therese, shivering as though she felt a violent chill.

She rose and grasped the water decanter.

"Let it be," exclaimed her husband, in a voice that he endeavoured to render natural, "I will prepare the sugar and water. You attend to your aunt."

He took the decanter of water from the hands of his wife and poured out a glassful. Then, turning half round, he emptied the contents of the small stoneware flagon into the glass at the same time as he dropped a lump of sugar into it. In the meanwhile, Therese had bent down before the sideboard, and grasping the kitchen knife sought to slip it into one of the large pockets hanging from her waist.

At the same moment, a strange sensation which comes as a warning note of danger, made the married couple instinctively turn their heads. They looked at one another. Therese perceived the flagon in the hands of Laurent, and the latter caught sight of the flash of the blade in the folds of the skirt of his wife.

For a few seconds they examined each other, mute and frigid, the husband near the table, the wife stooping down before the sideboard. And they understood. Each of them turned icy cold, on perceiving that both had the same thought. And they were overcome with pity and horror at mutually reading the secret design of the other on their agitated countenances.

Madame Raquin, feeling the catastrophe near at hand, watched them with piercing, fixed eyes.

Therese and Laurent, all at once, burst into sobs. A supreme crisis undid them, cast them into the arms of one another, as weak as children. It seemed to them as if something tender and sweet had awakened in their breasts. They wept, without uttering a word, thinking of the vile life they had led, and would still lead, if they were cowardly enough to live.

Then, at the recollection of the past, they felt so fatigued and disgusted with themselves, that they experienced a huge desire for repose, for nothingness. They exchanged a final look, a look of thankfulness, in presence of the knife and glass of poison. Therese took the glass, half emptied it, and handed it to Laurent who drank off the remainder of the contents at one draught. The result was like lightning. The couple fell one atop of the other, struck down, finding consolation, at last, in death. The mouth of the young woman rested on the scar that the teeth of Camille had left on the neck of her husband.

The corpses lay all night, spread out contorted, on the dining-room floor, lit up by the yellow gleams from the lamp, which the shade cast upon them. And for nearly twelve hours, in fact until the following day at about noon, Madame Raquin, rigid and mute, contemplated them at her feet, overwhelming them with her heavy gaze, and unable to sufficiently gorge her eyes with the hideous sight.

CPSIA information can be obtained at www.ICGtesting.com
Printed in the USA
LVOW110524190412

278254LV00001B/31/P